About the Authors

 **Leta Herman** is a writer, teacher of the Five Elements and Chinese Medicine, and a nationally certified acupressure practitioner. She has immersed herself in the philosophies of Daoism, Alchemical Healing, and Chinese Medicine, as well as many other healing modalities. Herman graduated from Smith College and has devoted the past fifteen years to learning everything possible about the Five Elements.

 **Jaye McElroy** is a writer, photographer, and business entrepreneur in Massachusetts and Rhode Island. She has completely integrated the Five Elements into her unique practice as a Five Element Life Coach. McElroy combines her career in advertising and business with the Five Elements to help people manifest their potential in life.

Get in touch with the authors at:
info@TheEnergyofLoveBook.com.

the energy of

L♥ve

APPLYING THE FIVE ELEMENTS TO TURN ATTRACTION INTO TRUE CONNECTION

LETA HERMAN & JAYE McELROY

Llewellyn Publications
Woodbury, Minnesota

FIRST EDITION
First Printing, 2014

Author photos: Leta Herman © Jaye McElroy
                 Jaye McElroy © nosleepzone.com
Book design by Bob Gaul
Cover design by Maria Garbe
Cover images © iStockphoto.com/831389/simonox
                iStockphoto.com/10725295/borisyankov
Interior illustrations by Llewellyn Art Department

Llewellyn Publications is a registered trademark of Llewellyn Worldwide Ltd.

Library of Congress Cataloging-in-Publication Data
Herman, Leta, 1967–
  The energy of love: applying the five elements to turn attraction into connection/
Leta Herman & Jaye McElroy.—First Edition.
    pages cm
  ISBN 978-0-7387-4019-5
  1. Love. 2. Intimacy (Psychology) I. Title.
  BF575.L8H44 2014
  177'.7—dc23
                       2013048977

Llewellyn Publications
A Division of Llewellyn Worldwide Ltd.
2143 Wooddale Drive
Woodbury, MN 55125-2989
www.llewellyn.com

Printed in the United States of America

Contents

Acknowledgments

We are deeply grateful to all who helped make this book come to life. Our heartfelt thanks go to Dr. Gail Herman, Dr. Steve Herman, and Cara Niederberger, our tireless editors who always said, "Bring it on," and "Who needs sleep anyway?" We also appreciate the many who reviewed their Elements: Kayla Solomon, Edith Adams Allison, Jessica Payne, Amanda Campbell, Dunan Herman-Parks, Elisia Langdon, Neal Parks, Leslie Lauf, and Genevieve Goetz. Don't worry ... your secrets are safe with us! Our thanks also go to the tireless sleeping (and snoring) at our feet provided by Ace, our number one doggie fan.

We also acknowledge Angela Wix and Bill Krause of Llewellyn for their help, guidance, and patience. We are grateful to Stephanie Abarbanel, who always took our calls with wonderfully keen advice. Also to Wendy Sherman—we are so grateful there are still nice people out in the world today. Special *shukran* to our smiling friends at Mosaic Café for their Moroccan rocket fuel tea that powered this book.

Leta

I am eternally grateful to Jaye for bringing her brilliant writing talent to this project. Her ability to be 100 percent engaged in everything made this book's creation fun and easy! She mastered the Five Elements faster and more thoroughly than anyone I've ever known, and her partnership in delivering this work has opened up my eyes to new ways the Five Elements can help all of us.

To my amazing teacher Jeffrey Yuen, who taught me with a wonderful sense of humor and clarity to open my mind as well as my heart to limitless possibilities. His wisdom was both healing and transformative at a key transition time in my life. Thanks also to my clients—my life teachers. Our one-on-one soul searching has brought so many "Aha" moments to understanding the Five Elements and the workings of each individual soul's search for authenticity.

Thanks to the many before me who dedicated their lives to the Five Elements: to J. R. Worsley, who brought the Five Element wisdom to the West; to Elizabeth Rochat de la Vallée and Claude Larre, whose improved translations of the ancient texts were instrumental to my understanding of the Five Elements; to Eliot Cowan, for introducing me to the Five Elements many years ago, and finally to Niki Bilton, who assimilated the teachings of many and took my understanding of the Five Elements to a whole new level.

To Dunan Herman-Parks for teaching me, "It's all good, Mom" every day of his beautiful life. Thanks to my parents, Gail and Steve Herman, for their unconditional Fire love. I've been so fortunate to know that I'm loved every day of my life. To Neal Parks for his dedication to everything I've become. To Sandra Hoover for her love and support over these many years.

To my friends Jill Goldreyer for pointing me on the healing path; Sally Hopkins Connor for being there for me from the start, my tour de force; and to all my friends all over the world for all the love, laughter, and positive energy you send every day. Thank you.

Jaye

I would like to thank everyone in my life for the constant support and encouragement to follow my life path, whatever that path may be. The joys in my life are so big and bold that they are everywhere I look.

Leta, Cara, Dax (and Ace)…The spark, the rock, and the barks.

Leta for asking me to share in this amazing project and making me laugh every day. Your light is so bright, the whole world can see it shining! Your brain works like no one I have ever met; you are inspiring! Thank you for helping me find my inner Yoda.

Cara Niederberger for being the most understanding, positive, loving person I will ever meet. Thank you, thank you, thank you.

Thanks to:

Panda, Dunan, Caitlin, Sarah, Amy, Adam Jr., Christopher, Willow, and Yara...for making me want to think about the future generations to come. I feel so much better about the world knowing you are all out there. To Mike and Janet Thomas for making me laugh so hard when we are together, my face hurts the next day. Amanda and Brent Campbell for being my kindred nerdy, crafting friends. We can so make that!

Gail and Steve Herman for their acceptance, love, and brilliant minds. Neal Parks, for being an amazing Artist in every sense of the word, and for being my "Metal" friend. My Nana, who told me at a very young age that I could do anything I wanted, and that I could decide my own destiny. Hard to understand at ten—brilliant now! My mother, Evelyn, for making me laugh even when I wanted to cry.

Introduction: Getting It?

Do you want it? Have you found it? Can you keep it?

What is "it"? Is it the love of your life? Is it steamy sex? Is it long-lasting connection and intimacy? In this book the "it" can be all of it ... it's what is right for you. It's your deepest desire at this moment in time. You know you want something. But you may not know exactly what "it" is!

The Energy of Love will help you clarify what you truly want in your relationship(s), how to find a lover who matches you energetically, and how to sustain a longer-lasting relationship while keeping sex and romance alive and well.

In this book, we use the ancient Chinese wisdom of the Five Elements to help you better understand love, sex, relationships, and much more. Once you discover your

Elemental Energy type, you'll learn how to find your perfect match for this time in your life. You can then start to let the Elements work for you in different kinds of relationships, including parent/child, work-related, and of course, love, sweet love!

In any relationship Energy is where the action really is (in and out of the bedroom!). Energy or *qi* in Chinese (also spelled *chi* and pronounced "chee") vibrates through us and out of us twenty-fours hours a day from cradle to grave. Energy is the one thing every living being on this planet has in common. Energy affects everyone around us.

Ancient Chinese Secret

Sometime in the past, about three thousand years ago, nobody knows exactly when, ancient Chinese scholars, philosophers, and physicians began documenting theories of the Five Elements—*Wood, Fire, Earth, Metal,* and *Water*—on human behavior and the nature of energy in the universe. The oldest surviving document of this type, called the *Huangdi Neijing* or the Yellow Emperor's Inner Canon, is two thousand years old and was first referenced in the year 111 CE. Now that's some shelf life!

The Five Elements don't only relate to love, they relate to everything, including the seasons of the year. They influence every aspect of life and even how people move. Every movement you make is influenced *energetically* by these Five Elements.

Many different interpretations and translations into English of the ancient Chinese Five Element texts have been compiled. Initial efforts to translate some of the Chinese words into English were difficult because the Chinese vocabulary regarding emotions is much more expansive than the English vocabulary. With the help of two famous Sinologists, Elizabeth Rochat de la Vallé and Claude Larre, both experts in translating Chinese into French and English, scholars are now discovering a much richer understanding of the Five Elements. These newer interpretations weren't included in many of the books written on the Five Elements—until now.

First Date Makeover

You can put away your magazine personality tests and astrological charts. No need to subject your prospective first date to a Myers-Briggs Type Indicator test to make sure you're compatible. Studying the Five Elements and knowing someone's Elemental Energy Type is a quick and easy way to discover what you want or don't want in romance. It's time to learn about energy and how two people can create a long-lasting love relationship.

Sharing the Knowledge

When we share this information with clients in our healing and coaching practices, they are blown away with how insightful and accurate the Five Elements are. Now, we want to share our knowledge, our personal interpretations, and our observations in a fun and lively way for everyone to enjoy. By reading *The Energy of Love*, we hope you get to know the Five Elements and all their nuances intimately (pun intended!).

Discovering Chinese Medicine was a major turning point in both our lives, and Leta has spent well over a decade seriously studying the subtle and technical details of how this all works. She's been applying her knowledge in her practice as an acupressurist and holistic healer. Jaye has developed a process for applying this knowledge in marketing and business and then putting an Elemental twist on motivational coaching.

People who study Chinese Medicine, Feng Shui, and even martial arts often hear something about the Five Elements. But many don't understand energy the way the ancient Chinese did. Both of us enjoy sharing this distinctive approach to understanding others and yourself in a way you can use in your everyday life, especially in your relationships.

We wrote this book to be entertaining, uplifting, and empowering with the same spirit we bring to every person we meet on a daily basis. If you want to have a better love relationship with yourself and others, you just have to have a desire to open your eyes to see the energy of the Five Elements vibrating all around you. You're on a lifelong journey—*your* life and journey—and it can be filled with excitement and fun if you let yourself be who you are truly meant to be.

One

Finders Keepers

....

"Love yourself first and everything falls into line."
Lucille Ball

....

If you asked a hundred people what love is, chances are you would get a hundred different answers. Everyone seems to have a different view on this universal topic because most people do not understand the *energetics* of love. What if we told you there was a much simpler reason why most relationships don't stand the test of time? We have found that the answer is actually quite simple. It is not about hot bodies, sexy jobs, or gorgeous hair—it's about energy! Yes, the magical ingredient that makes love and sex sizzle is the same thing that makes it fizzle and wilt right before your eyes. "Energy" is a little six-letter word that represents a force more powerful than anything in the universe. Heck, it's what runs the universe!

Is love *just* a chemical state in our minds? Or, is it a manufactured concept to sell Hollywood movie tickets and chocolates? How about almost every pop song ever written? All about love, love, love. Good love, bad love, lost love, found love, falling in, falling out... Perhaps you think love is a random act that just happens to a lucky few who spontaneously gaze into each other's eyes at exactly the right moment in time (add your favorite romantic music for that special effect).

You may not understand what love is, but you know how it feels... an intense, almost instant attraction that makes tingly sensations wake up inside you. Is it their looks? Is it the glint in their eyes? Their smile? The way they hold their body as they walk? The sound of their voice? Or maybe it's their secret, sneaky pheromones you don't even know you're smelling that turn you on? You *have to* find out more about this individual. You *need* to find out more. For some reason, you are just *into* this person.

You might not be able to explain what love is, but you know when you're in it. Stripping away the Hollywood veneers, sugary pop-song lyrics, and sappy greeting cards, we can actually look at what is really going on between lovers. What do *you* think love is?

Why Settle?

Sometimes we may get distracted by appearances, such as the person's looks, how they dress, where they went to school, what they do for work, or where they live and play. These are all superficial, materialistic things and have nothing to do with *who* that person really is and whether you're both really compatible.

Things may be great at the beginning of a romance, but when love suddenly goes bad faster than an egg-salad sandwich left out on the picnic blanket in July, you just want to figure out why. What did *I* do wrong? What did *they* do wrong? Why can't it stay good? Why does it have to change? Why? Why? Why?

You search for the deciding event that may have caused the dimming of the spark—a wandering eye, crazy parents, the ex that won't move on—whatever you can think of to make yourself feel better. You just can't figure out what or when or where the relationship went wrong. Some people simply realize over time they are not in love anymore, or never really were in love.

Are you always waiting for something to end the relationship, always waiting for the other shoe (the bad one) to drop? Have we built a whole culture based on sex and sizzle when maybe we should be focused on compatibility, love, and compassion?

Relationships are like trying to find a station on a car radio. When the scanner hits the right frequency, the music comes through loud and clear. Goodbye static; hello music, sweet music!

Most of us won't put up with a bad radio station for more than a minute or two. However, (for those of you old enough to remember life before smartphones) if you've ever driven a long lonely stretch of road for hours and hours with no good stations, you might settle for a bad station out of desperation.

Is this how you want to approach finding a lover? A partner? A romantic relationship? If you've been driving love's lonely road for too long, do you really want to settle out of desperation for a lot of annoying static just because she's "a good person" or he's "a nice guy"? Let's face it—he might be nice, but if you're just not tuning into his frequency, why would you continue? And yet, that's what happens in a lot of cases. We hear over and over from people who still can't decide if their lover is *right* for them, sometimes after twenty-five years of marriage.

Our culture is in crisis about love. We think finding Mr. or Ms. Right is so rare, elusive, and nearly impossible. So, many times, we grab the first person who looks half-way decent and don't let go! Have we gotten lazy in the love department? Have we lost our faith in true love? Do we even know how to find satisfying love?

Good Vibrations

The Elemental Energy of you mixes and mingles with the energy of every other person you meet. Your Element makes your voice sound the way it does. It makes you walk a certain way. It influences the look in your eyes and how you see the world. You even have your own unique smell that can attract or repel certain types of people.

You might be casually talking to the cashier at the grocery store, and your energies collide. You may feel an instant liking—a breath of fresh air. Or maybe the meeting feels like nothing at all, no big deal, like a cosmic fog drifting together, in which case you just move on through your day. These interactions are influenced by the Elemental Energies of everyone you meet. This happens over and over, day after day for your entire life, start to finish.

If you know what Elemental Energy type you are and what Element your lover is, you can understand if this romance is right for you at this time in your life, or not. Discovering this early in a relationship really puts the odds of success in your favor. Or, if you have been struggling in a longer relationship, what if you could *really* understand your partner's Elemental needs and start to love again in a way you both can enjoy each other? If you know how to pick a compatible Elemental Energy type, love could thrive, grow, and be exciting once more. And sex can be as wild or tame as you desire!

High Five!

You can think of the Five Elements as movement. Each Element describes a fundamental type of movement through time and space. *Wood* surges forward and quickly retreats. *Fire* bounces up and down. *Earth* moves circularly. *Metal* descends. *Water* moves forward without stopping.

This book will teach you to easily identify most people's Element by watching them walk and listening to them talk. You will then have powerful tools to understand your current partner or future lovers in a whole new light. If you determine a person's Elemental Energy type, you can almost predict how they will act and respond. The payoffs are worthwhile!

Think about it. If you had the power to make people feel at ease from the moment you met, and if you knew how they were going to react to you, how would that help you in your life? Buying a car, getting a bank loan, impressing your boss, rocking that first date of a new romance—the list is endless. Knowing how to use these powerful tools, you can adjust energetically to anyone in your life. You can connect in a positive and powerful way.

Once you've learned about each of the Five Elements, the rest of this book will start to explore how the Five Elements can help bring love and romance into your life. When you meet someone who turns you on, you may be physically attracted to them or have something in common that feels exciting. You may want to rush into getting to know this person. But if you know your Elemental Energy type, the process of getting to know each other can be much more rewarding. You can quickly understand who this person *really* is and whether they are compatible with you. Later in chapter nine, we explain the three types of relationships in the Five Elements: those that are the same energetic type (such as Metal/Metal, Fire/Fire), those with different but compatible energies (such as Wood/Fire, Metal/Water), and those with opposite energies (such as Earth/Wood, Water/Fire). You can avoid a lot of misunderstandings that arise from simply having different energetic styles by understanding the dynamics of these three types of relationships.

What will you do with this new, exciting relationship? Will you nourish, respect, and embrace it in a way that allows you both to grow and change in a healthy way? Or will you cling to the person like a life raft, then suck all the air out, trying to keep the relationship the same, fearing you may lose your lover if either of you changes in any way, shape, or form?

Even though your Elemental type remains the same from the day you were born to the day you die, your perspective may change as your life unfolds before you. As you travel on your journey, your life changes, your heart changes, your needs change. You do not view the world the same as when you were a young child, a college student, or even later in life. Your needs were different before you had children. Most definitely your needs change after you've raised your children. You go through different stages of change. Change is inevitable, change is good!

Don't Get Shortchanged

What we are here to say is, it's totally acceptable to want more out of your relationships as you move through life. Reach out for the relationship that is in alignment with who you really are at this moment in your life. Later in chapter ten you'll learn about the different stages of your needs in relationships based on your Elemental Energy type.

You deserve to find that true connection so that you can joyfully share experiences in this wonderful world. Love can take many forms, but we all need it somewhere in our lives—it is a universal need for all beings. In order to find true connection, we can tell you one thing early on; you must first connect with the most perfect person of all—*yourself!* We want you to fall in love with yourself, to seek out and find your bliss and a love that is deep inside you. That might sound kind of corny and sticky sweet, but it is the core of what discovering and understanding the Five Elements in yourself is about. Embracing who you really are is about discovering who you really are.

The more you love yourself and are in love with life, the more ready you'll be to meet someone who is putting out the same kind of vibe. So with that said, the first step to finding your true love is to be happy with who you are right now, in this very stage of your life. We believe that in order to experience deep, fulfilling love, you must find, understand, and embrace your true identity—by accepting who you are Elementally and being authentic. Oh, if it was only that easy! Well, the Five Elements can help you accept yourself, accept your lover, and embrace the differences. Being authentic … now *that* is a beautiful thing.

People throughout your life may have spent a lot of time trying to convince you to not be authentically yourself. What? Really? Yes, they want you to be just like them. They may not openly admit that, but it is true time and time again. Parents, grandparents, lovers, employers—all these people may want you to be someone you're not, some unconsciously, others consciously try to change you. It is also very likely that at some point in your life you've tried to help others by wanting them to be more like you.

So many people travel down that road of trying to change their partners or lovers to fit into what they want or need. The truth is that if you change temporarily to make someone else happy, you might lose yourself and could become depressed or ill. You may find it very hard to get back to your true self if you get lost trying to always please another person. Trying to change to fit your partner's needs whether or not it is the right match is so hard and exhausting for both of you.

Sage Advice

There is an authentic way to be yourself. The Chinese masters of old believed that your Elemental Energy type dictates what you want most in life. They believed in reincarnation and called these your "lessons" that you would strive to complete during this lifetime on Earth. They also believed that once you've completed your life lessons, you become a Sage or a highly evolved person, even immortal! In order to follow this path and truly evolve, you need to understand and fulfill the purpose of your own Element (which never changes in this lifetime) plus that of all the other Elements.

Learning and understanding the Five Elements will allow you the chance to come into alignment with your higher self, what the ancient Chinese call your "Spirit Level." Daoists have the concept of a divine, universal energy called the *dao* or Source. It's a little like what "God" means to those in the West. We will use the term "Divine" in this book. Your Spirit Level is the Divine's presence in you.

The Chinese believe that aligning with your Spirit Level is a great achievement on the path to enlightenment. They believe the first step is to release self-judgment and accept yourself. It is ancient and old and totally relevant in today's new age concept of thinking—it's really mind-boggling that they figured this out over three thousand years ago. Don't worry… you don't have to understand all the intricacies of ancient Chinese Medicine to get the benefit of the wisdom. That would be impossible. We, as contemporary individuals, can take from the ancients what is relevant to our lives today so that we can thrive and move through life in a much more powerful and loving way.

The Five Elements give us a framework for understanding ourselves and how we love. If you and your lover can understand what truly motivates you in love, then your relationship can withstand the changes in the outer world as well as the changes in your own hearts. When you understand the growth path of each Element and you learn how to be authentic in yourselves, you can help each other evolve and change in a supportive, loving way.

Many long-term married couples have asked us for help to find out what has happened to their relationship. We discuss how to heal longer relationships at the end of this book in chapter eleven. Together, a couple can work to rediscover not only what they once loved about each other, but also what they love about themselves. If you're hoping to return back from the land of the lost with a long-term partner, both of you will need to work to rekindle the love and embrace change.

Love can be quite a roller coaster ride when you have someone who is the opposite of your energy, like Fire and Water. There can be a huge attraction in opposites, but a lot of friction as well. You can accept and be honest about these differences and find solutions that honor both ways of being without trying to change the other person. Or you may realize that the difference is so great that neither of you wants to find compromise. In that case, you can walk away from such a relationship without blame or anger if you accept your energetic differences.

When you are authentic and true to yourself, you will receive all that you want. When you understand your needs and are living in the moment—that is the ultimate way to live.

Okay, let's not wait any longer. Let's get started, seat belts off, hands outside the safety zone, throw all those cautions right into that big ol' wind, 'cause here we go … you are going to learn how to have the freedom to fly in your life. Hopefully, when you are finished with this book you will fall in love with the most amazing person you have ever met—YOU!

We hope you find this as fascinating as we do. You are holding the keys to your own life, so start your engines, please.

Two

Turn It Up,
Turn Me On!

....

*"You know you're in love when you can't fall asleep
because reality is finally better than your dreams."*

Dr. Seuss

....

When you're turned on, something amazing happens in
your body. What exactly is that amazing burst of energy
in all the right places? Wow! Ka-pow!

You know the feeling—when someone you're attracted
to is in close proximity to you, it feels like electricity being
turned on all over your body, almost like this power surge
has a mind of its own. Zing!

It seemingly just happens, or so we think. The healers of ancient China had a simple explanation for this phenomenon—they believed your body is an energy system and that energy, called qi, runs through it. You can't see or touch it, but it's there because you feel it inside you. We feel our own life force when we are energized by life.

Tiny Love Tendrils, Oh My!

Your energy system has tiny love tendrils that extend out from your heart all over your body like an electric grid, responding physically to things you like. This is your mojo, your sex appeal. It wakes up your body, speeds up your breathing, raises your temperature, and causes you to be suddenly alert—it plugs you in and turns you on. The Chinese gave every organ of the body an "official" name. And for this function of the heart, they gave it the name "the Circulation Sex Official." Now that's a name!

These feelings aren't reserved just for sexual attraction to people. You might feel it when you're passionate about anything—things you really love to do, such as dancing, singing, creating music and art, eating amazing food, and playing intense sports. In other words, you can be excited for life. This excitement and heightened energy level is what attracts others to you.

Yet, life is not always so easy. Our energies are not always flowing at maximum levels. When we feel super tired, weighed down by life, or hurt by mean people, and our hearts are closed, we feel more like zombies than sexy or red hot lovers. When our hearts shut down to the meanness of the world, they don't send out those energy signals to our bodies, and we aren't plugged in. Our tiny love tendrils lie dormant and quiet. This could be the point in your relationship when you start to choose sleep over sex!

Say Chi-eese

Our energy plays a much bigger role in love than we think. Most of us don't realize that when we interact with someone, our energies mix and mingle in ways that don't have to do with the words we speak. Body language, the sounds of our voices, the look in our eyes, even our smell can all be appealing or appalling. Sometimes we can be very attracted to someone's energy, or we might have a strong aversion to it. Yes, it goes both ways.

The Chinese believe there are five types of energy movement in the universe. These are called the Five Elements. And these energies have attraction and aversion forces, like magnets pulling each other together or polar opposites pushing each other apart.

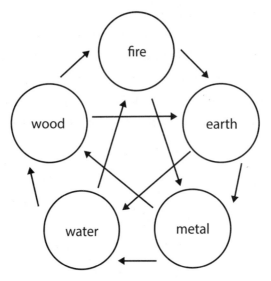

Figure 1—The Five Elements

The Five Elements				
Wood	Fire	Metal	Water	Earth
Spring	Summer	Autumn	Winter	Transitions
Bursting forth energy that springs up and out.	Blooming and maturing energy that says "ta-da!" to the world.	Floating downward energy, like leaves falling from trees.	Forward movement, like a river rushing to the sea.	Circular energy, like being enveloped in a big hug.

A simple way to understand the Five Elements is to think of the seasons they represent. "But," you say, "there are four seasons!" So true! There are four seasons and Five Elements. How does that work? Easy. The fifth season, so to speak, is the transitions between all the seasons—the Earth Element. All seasons need to gradually transition into the next, and transitions are the Earth Element's job.

- *Wood* is like spring energy. It is a bursting forth energy that springs up and out.

- *Fire* is summer energy—a blooming and maturing energy that says "ta-da!" to the world.

- *Metal* is a floating downward energy like the leaves falling from the trees in autumn.

- *Water* is winter energy that alternates between stillness, like a pond, and sudden movement and power, like a tsunami. But mostly it moves forward, never stopping, like a river.

- *Earth* energy is circular in nature. It's like getting a big hug. It's associated with the transitions between all the seasons, and is best represented by the harvest season in later summer because it's the time we receive all the bounty of summer and share it with our friends.

Primary and Secondary Elements— Who's on First (and Second)?

By now, you may be wondering which Element you are. In truth, you are all Five Elements. Every person, animal, and even plant has the ability to move with any of the Five Element energies. However, the belief is that each being on the planet has one Element that is predominant. You were born this way, and this Element gives you the purpose of your life. Everything you do is guided by your Element, though it's not dictated by the month you are born, as in astrology. It's like a default behavior that you have when you're not trying to do or be something else. And the original Five Element theories indicate that you're more likely to have the same energy as one of your parents. Occasionally, people are not like either parent's Elemental Energy types.

Your secondary Element is your backup plan in life. It's the energetic type you use when your primary Element doesn't quite cut it socially. As humans we are very social creatures and rely on social cues to fit in (or not) to certain situations. We also rely on our second Elements a lot in relationships because we often pick friends and lovers whose primary Element is our secondary Element, which helps compatibility.

We continuously adapt to all different social situations as we move through life. You should only need to access your second Element about fifteen percent of the time. In a perfect world, you want to be comfortable living in your first Element most of the time. Let's say you love to laugh and socialize with people. You might be Fire. So maybe your primary Element makes you too loud to be, let's say, in a library, where quiet is the norm and expected. So you draw upon a second Element (hopefully an Element that's able to be quieter or more contained, for example, Earth or Metal) when entering the building.

Luckily most of us can switch to our second Element quite easily. Note that we said "most of us," as there are always the exceptions to this rule. We all know them and see them on a regular basis . . . that one person who can't shift or adapt. They usually stand out, and people feel obliged to encourage or shame them back into compliance with social norms.

Third Element—Drama Queens and Kings

"Woe is me. Life stinks. I stink. You stink. We all stink." Drama, drama, drama . . . Your third Element is about your nightmare situations. It's what we like to call, your "drama spot."

We've all been there. Thankfully we only have to use this Element about five percent of the time in our lives. Sick as a dog for two weeks in bed? Yes, that'll do it. The love of your life dumps you for your best friend? There it is again. Get fired from your favorite job without notice? Ugh, that totally stinks! Hello, drama spot.

You will most likely default to that third Element when life finds you at its most miserable. Whatever the catastrophe, disaster, or bad times, it's that rock-bottom, down-and-out place we all have felt at some point in our lives—that is where your third Element comes into play.

The third Element is about how you handle those situations. What story do you tell yourself when you're really down? Each of the Five Element types has an unhappy story associated with it, and it's your third Element that dictates which of those stories you tell at these times. People who have the Wood Element third might say to themselves (angrily), "This is so not fair!" Fire as the third Element might say (sadly), "No one really loves me!" Earth as a third Element could exclaim (whiningly), "No one ever helps me when I need it!" Metal third might state (pathetically), "No one ever respects me." Lastly, a Water third person might say (dramatically), "I am totally exhausted! I just need to lie down!" The third Element, when activated, helps you find your way back to yourself in difficult times. You need to rest desperately, so you do. Life is good again. Yay!

So while you have the ability to be all five, you have a specific mix of the Elements. For example, you might be Fire/Earth/Wood/Metal/Water, which would most likely make you a very active social person who enjoys attending many special events and occasions. Or you might be Wood/Water/Metal/Fire/Earth, and be a very driven, no nonsense, let's get-stuff-done kind of person. Each combination of the Five Elements is different and somewhat unique. And by the way, if you're bristling about being too similar to other people, Metal and Wood people don't like to be categorized or labeled, whereas Fire and Earth people love to be included and understood. Water will usually ignore you and chuckle at your attempts to figure them out.

What Element Am I?

What's most important is for you to understand your *first* Element. You can learn to embrace who you truly are and what motivates you in love and life. This book will help you understand the nature of energy and how it connects or disconnects you from others. Once you learn your Element, you will understand better what you need or desire from love. This may give you a better chance of creating a connected relationship with a sizzling sex life as a bonus!

First we need to help you determine which Element you are. Each of the next five chapters explains one of the Five Elements. As you read each one, be open-minded and honest with yourself. Does it feel like your core nature? Is it similar? Which do you resonate with?

There are three easy ways to identify a person's Elemental Energy type: the Walk, the Talk, and the Look. Each Elemental type has a specific kind of walk, a specific sound of the voice, and a particular look in the eyes that characterizes it. As we introduce each Element in depth, we will focus on these three ways to identify a person's Elemental type.

Each Element also has specific personality descriptions that are explained in detail. Every person is unique. Not everyone will fit the bill of their Element exactly, but most everyone resonates with a very large percentage of their Elemental traits. There will always be a few exceptions depending on your developmental years and childhood circumstances. No worries, if you are truly honest with yourself, your Elemental energies will reveal themselves in time.

Three

Wood— Got Wood?

....

"You can have it all. Just not all at once."
Oprah Winfrey

....

Are you, as a lover, someone who craves real connection with your partner on a high energy, multi-faceted Mr. Toad's Wild Ride adventure? Do you want someone who loves to have fun doing many different things in life and in love? Are you someone who feels safe knowing that someone's got your back? Then read on, because you might be one of the movers and shakers of the world—a decision-maker. If you are nodding your head "yes," then baby, you've got Wood!

Walk This Way...

The way you hold your energy in your body as you walk into a room makes everyone take notice of your arrival. Woods walk with their chest out and head held high, oozing confidence and charisma. You may feel a little shy inside, but that's not what the world sees! The world only sees your assertive, bold side. Many people find these key attributes sexy, stimulating, and very desirable in a partner.

At social gatherings, do you know how to work the room, make the right connections, and network whenever possible? Do you find yourself going from group to group, starting conversations with the guests, rocking their worlds, and moving on, hopefully leaving people wanting just a little more of you? Are your comebacks witty and immediate? Do you love to be the punster? Do you arrive late to social gatherings to avoid the slow (and boring) beginnings because you know the party doesn't really start until a big Wood arrives? Do you leave parties early to avoid the dragged out (and boring) endings? Do you hate being boring and are all about action? Do you even hate the word "boring"? Are you already skimming ahead in this book? If you are answering "yes," "yes," "yes," and mostly "yes" to these questions, well, it looks like you have Wood as your first element, my friend. Keep reading and maybe—just maybe—we can show you something you might not have known about yourself or your romantic interest.

Do you almost always wear at least one conversation-starting article of clothing? Maybe sport a funky new hairdo or creatively groomed beard or mustache that you change frequently? What about colorful ties, socks, or purses?

When they're in the mood to socialize, Wood can elevate a party to a whole new level. If not at a party, then at a business meeting, an afternoon ball game, or yes, even a romantic date—they exude a confidence whenever and wherever they go. They are magnets, attracting people to their power and strength. Charismatic charmers, they know how to make anyone feel good. In fact, it's their role in life to be the cheerleader for the rest of us. Too cocky? Too arrogant? Too over-the-top confident? People may perceive them as that, but Wood doesn't see themselves that way. They feel they are genuine and self-assured ... traits that mostly come naturally to them. It is not that they don't work at their skills, because they do. They just get better and better.

Power Player in the Boardroom and the Bedroom

Wood exemplifies the traditional idea of the successful role model in American business—a strong, bold, assertive, and fearless leader. They love a good challenge, the bigger the better. They prefer to delegate, but they're not afraid to work hard even in the trenches if needed to get the job done. As master negotiators and big decision-makers, they are likely to get the upper hand in every deal. Donald Trump, Wood.

Warren Buffet, Wood. Steve Jobs, Wood. These are all strong men who have wielded their skills in the business world.

In 2013, a whole crop of strong Wood women took powerful roles in leading today's top businesses such as Indra Nooyi of Pepsico, Irene Rosenfeld of Kraft, and Oprah Winfrey who runs her own TV network OWN, to just name a few.

Hillary Clinton is a great example of a Wood woman rocking the world of politics with her strengths. Rachel Maddow (Wood) is talking smart politics nightly on her own TV show on MSNBC. These are smart women who are not afraid to speak their minds and exert their influence over others.

Hollywood Gets Wood

Hollywood's leading men are big in the Wood department. Think George Clooney, Brad Pitt, Tom Cruise, Sean Penn, and Ryan Gosling ... Wood, Wood, Wood, Wood, and sexy Wood. Yep, these Hollywood heavyweights all have Wood as their first Element.

Bruce Willis? Totally Wood. Arnold Schwarzenegger? Big Wood. Robert Downey Jr., ironclad Wood. These men play strong, action-seeking heroes who also know how to love the ladies. That is Wood ... Audiences love these traits and Hollywood knows it! Let's not leave out comedians George Carlin, Will Ferrell, Jon Stewart, and Stephen Colbert, also Wood men.

In the past, Wood women in Hollywood may have had a tougher time being strong when they were expected to appear weak and demure on the screen. That didn't stop actresses like Bette Davis, Katharine Hepburn, Lauren Bacall, and Jodie Foster from paving the road for other Wood women today to play powerful characters. In today's society, Wood women are now praised for being leaders and role models.

Oprah, Ellen, Madonna, Lady Gaga, Pink!, Tina Fey, Jennifer Lopez ... Yes, all strong Wood women! Talk about the Hollywood A-List, how about a W-List for Wood!

The trail-blazing show *Murphy Brown* in the 1980s showed us that a Wood woman can make it in a man's world. Candice Bergen as Murphy Brown showed the world that a woman could be both beautiful and strong. Okay, for you younger readers, Tina Fey, the first woman head writer on *Saturday Night Live* and creator of *30 Rock* is another great example of a Wood woman on TV. Her recent book *Bossy Pants* describes her lifelong Wood-like follies. We could as easily call her *Smarty Pants* and *Woody Pants*. Okay, that doesn't really sound great, but you get the idea and hopefully a nice chuckle.

Wood singers, actresses, and entertainers are attractive because they are clearly in control and hold their own power as beacons of light shining out for all to see. *Saturday Night Live* alumnae Tina Fey and Amy Poehler as well as comedian Kathy Griffin are leading the way for comedic Wood women in the world today. All these smart Wood women are rocking their worlds—and ours.

Wood is quick witted, engages the world, and focuses on fun activities. But some other characteristics include feeling very strongly about justice and fairness in the world. Woods often feel it's their duty to protect those who are vulnerable in the world, such as mistreated animals and children. Or they may feel they've been unfairly treated and can become quite angry and bitter about it.

The Remover of Obstacles

Woods might not be incredibly nurturing, but they do remove obstacles to help other people accomplish their greatness. They are great motivators and coaches. Both men and women Wood are the ultimate cheerleaders for the rest of the world. Think of them as the Tony Robbinses of the world. Tony of course is the ultimate Wood coach. Go Tony! Yeah.

How does Wood remove obstacles for themselves and others? Well, for one, they don't take no for an answer. No means yes! They find any means necessary to reach the big vision. Some see problems in life; Wood views them as challenges.

Second, they think outside the box. They expand people's horizons. Third, they like to help people achieve their goals. Win-win is a strong theme with Wood. They love to win, and they like to see people they care about reach their dreams.

They've accomplished many things. They've been the team captains, class officers, business leaders, head writers, and pro-athletes. Whatever they're good at, they excel at it. They already embody greatness! They are natural born leaders.

Why do they want to help people? Because they've spent their entire lives working to be the very best they can be and want to help others to realize their potential. Why? Because sometimes it's lonely at the top! Wood wants to engage, and if no one is playing at their level, or close, it is not fun for Wood. Life can be boring or lonely. Wood hates the b-word, which is *boring*.

Wood Burns for Love

Wood loves a challenge in general, and the conquest of love is no exception. As with any contest, Wood loves the thrill of pursuing a goal. Once Wood wins your love, the question is, are you able to hold their interest for long enough to create a lasting relationship? If not, they're likely to move on to the next challenge.

However, let's not make them seem disloyal or shallow. Once they make a commitment to something, or someone, Woods can be some of the most loyal partners on the planet. This may mean they stick with a bad marriage or bad romance a lot longer than is good for either person. They persist because they hate the idea of throwing in the towel or possibly being called a quitter.

Sometimes a conflict exists between Wood's constant need for newness in their lives, their kindness and desire to be good, and the expectations of faithfulness in a traditional relationship. Sometimes Wood is shocked to be caught up in an affair while still in a more traditional relationship, such as marriage. And because Woods are so smart, they can sometimes get away with an affair, if they want. But the guilt might weigh on their conscience (they have a strong sense of doing what's right), and they end up revealing the truth to all parties in the end.

It's not that they wanted to end their marriage or ruin their relationships. It's just that they live for newness in their life. They represent the dawn and a new day. One thing that's sure about Wood; they are guaranteed to change, and change often. While Wood prefers to be with one person at a time, some of the new beliefs about open relationships that have emerged in recent times can be quite appealing, as long as they are socially acceptable and agreed upon by all parties. Even though they like to push the boundaries of what can be done, and sometimes bend the rules if they appear unfair, they don't ever want to feel like social outcasts. They prefer to be the ones that everyone else can look up to, which is sometimes someone who blazes new trails!

Wood likes to please. They want their lovers to be happy. They can be over-achievers or perfectionists in the romance department. They can do big romance if they want to woo someone, like renting a stretch limo, lifting off for a date in a hot-air balloon, or proposing at a football game on the digital scoreboard for all to see. They like to make a big impression, like big shots. Think Frank Sinatra big! Wood does big.

Do you want to attract a Wood lover into your life? If you're attracted to strength, quick wit, and charisma, it's likely you're at a time in your life when you want to be with a strong, capable person. Woods often are so accomplished that they can take care of those around them. They don't mind so long as they're not being taken advantage of or being exploited. Or maybe you want to be a strong, capable person, excelling to greatness, and you just need that expert cheerleader by your side. Wood is that Element.

Let the Sex Games Begin!

Sex with Wood is always new and different…interesting, stimulating, and challenging. It involves engagement, laughter, sweat, and give and take. You don't just lie there. At the end, you may feel like you've gone for a run or worked out at the gym. Woods are natural athletes and love to work hard, even in bed!

They want to feel that they've done a good job satisfying their partner. They also want to find the best lover/partner. They aim high, as with everything else in their lives. Wood wants the perfect partner, lover, or romantic interest…every time, all the time.

Since Woods mostly have some kind of goal with everything they do, the goal might be to please their lover. Or it might be a goal within themselves, to achieve something through orgasm they've never achieved before or to reach some spiritual height.

That said, they are likely to have a quieter side that makes them be very soft and cuddly. People in the world only see the strong, assertive, outer Wood, not seeing the hidden inner tenderness. Woods crave peace and quiet when they're not so big out in the world. They value their privacy and like to do a lot of projects at home. They can be extremely gentle and love to snuggle when they're in the mood. This soft part is their secret that they only show to their lover.

But don't ever mistake their softness for weakness. Don't ever call your Wood partner weak! Don't even THINK that word in their presence. If Wood feels weak, they are severely and dangerously depressed, which only happens when they've met an obstacle they've been banging their head against and can't overcome. If Wood gives up, it is not a pretty picture, but is luckily rare.

They love to try new things and be innovative. They want to play. Sex with Wood isn't boring—one day it might be a new position, funky music, or an unusual location. Whatever it is, it's sure to be new and creative. Such is the life with a Wood partner. Embrace their way of life, and it can be a fun and thrilling ride! If sex with a Wood is boring, something is wrong with the relationship. Wood might only be in the relationship out of a sense of loyalty or not wanting to give up. It's time to seriously evaluate your relationship to see whether both partners can reinvigorate the inventiveness that was present at the beginning of the union.

Joining the A-Team

Wood loves their partners for their best qualities and their potential for growth. So it's not healthy for your relationship with Wood to be down on yourself. They don't want to dwell on your faults. They want to overlook them and focus on what they love about you. And they want you to love them for the same reasons. Everyone loves to be loved. But when Wood asks, "Why do you love me?" they want to know if you *see* their greatness.

What specifically is great about them? What do you see in them that makes you love them? How are they different (and better) than others you may have loved before? And they certainly don't want to hear you love them even though you think they're messing up. That's a total downer for Wood. They never see loss in the world, only winning. So they don't want their partner to ever see them as having failed or lost.

If they have indeed lost a game or made a big mistake…hmmm…well, clearly *that* doesn't happen very often. But let's just say they are already keenly aware of when they've, ahem, "lost." They don't need you to point out that fact. It's Wood's job to find the "win" in every game. You'll hear them tell their teammates how well they played despite the loss. When they lose, you need to see how great they were in the game's playing or strategy and not concentrate on the actual outcome if it was less than desirable.

If you want to *play* with Wood, you will need to be totally engaged. You need to be smart, which means keeping up with the Wood level of cleverness. This isn't the kind of smarts you learn from books or getting an advanced degree. The essential ingredients are a quick wit and the ability to think on your toes. Wood also wants someone who appreciates their creativity and brilliance (though they easily laugh at themselves as well). And they constantly invite you to step up to their level. They want you to be on the A-team with them.

They are incredibly impatient. Bureaucracy is the kiss of death. Waiting in lines is like nails on the blackboard for Wood. They frantically think of everything wrong with the situation, like, "Where'd all these people come from, and why are they not at work?" or "Why don't they hire more people?" "If their services were better, we wouldn't have to even come here," they might think in frustration. Their big Wood heads want to explode with the frustration over the lack of efficiency! It just drives them crazy.

One such Wood recently told the story of when he went to his local cable TV office and the line was out the door with only one person working at the window. So ... instead of waiting in the seemingly endless and senseless line, the Wood guy offered someone closer to the front of the line twenty dollars to trade places. Twenty dollars evidently was not enough, so he then proceeded to the front of the line and offered a woman (with two small children in tow) fifty dollars for her slot. She accepted his offer and simply walked to the back of the line. He was the next person called for help. They both were happy. Win-win—it's the Wood way!

In a romantic relationship, Wood needs someone who moves and adapts quickly. Woods can be like race cars that need high maintenance. They can be very picky, for example, about food and comfort. If they seem to require a lot of maintenance, it's because they are capable of moving so fast through life. You also need to be able to laugh to be with Wood because they have incredible wit and love to laugh. They seek someone who understands the way that Wood sees the world—outside the box. It's as if Wood is constantly turning things upside down to see a new vantage point.

Wood can't tolerate boring conversations (there's that dreaded b-word again). If you take five minutes to describe how you made your breakfast that morning, there's no chance for a relationship—unless you're riffing on creative and humorous new ways to make toast! As one Wood recently said, "He was so boring, it was like vanilla pudding without the vanilla!"

Good Wood Gone Bad

Wood comes with a ton of great qualities, plus a few that are less than desirable. These are what we like to call the challenges for Wood in the romance and relationship department.

For example, if you are Wood and struggling in life, you might not recognize yourself as much fun. You may feel beaten down or you're embroiled in a difficult situation. Normally you find ways to overcome hardship, but it's not always easy for your partner to watch. Winning is always paramount. Wood in battle is focused 100 percent on winning. It's hard for Wood to feel romantic when in such a situation.

Whenever Wood is feeling frustrated all day long, something has to shift. It's time to play a new game. Perhaps you're embroiled in a bad divorce. Well, the justice system is one huge, slow-moving bureaucratic nightmare for Wood. And there's little you can do to quickly outsmart it. Since Woods hate losing or waiting, it's time to do something radical that has nothing to do with a soon-to-be ex. It's time to take a road trip, get a motorcycle, or go study watercolor painting in Paris. It's time to have fun playing a new game that you can win at!

So when does the lover's honeymoon end for Wood? It's the day their lover starts criticizing them. They are totally okay with growing and being a better person, but they do that from a place of *already winning*. If their partner sees them losing or doing something wrong (all the time), either they shut down or have to move on.

If you want to make a suggestion for change, perhaps first tell your Wood lover what they're doing right. Then say, "Honey, I think what you did was amazing. Next time, can we try it a little differently so it can be even better?" You can help them re-strategize better ways of connecting and winning, together as a team. Excellence is the theme. They can take suggestions if made in a way that is for the good of the relationship and not an attack on them. Yes, it's true Wood does need a little coddling every now and then—a little tune-up every once in a while keeps that high-performance race car running perfectly.

Against the Grain

Wood has no problem with reflecting on past actions and figuring out better ways to do it in the future. There's no criticism in that. It's about strategy, flexibility, and adaptability. You can use past experiences (but not past lovers) to create better and better ways of doing things in the romance department. And like a strong tree on the cliff in a storm, Wood can bend in the wind and still survive. Whenever Wood becomes stubborn or rigid, they lose their flexibility and sense of humor. It's not pretty, especially for their partners, who can often take the brunt of the frustration. When Wood is off, everyone around them knows it. There are exclamations of exasperation all day long. The old saying, "If *so and so* is not happy, no one is happy" clearly refers to Wood having a bad day!

If Wood is arguing with you, the simplest and best question to ask is, "What do you think is the best way to resolve the problem?" Then listen to what they have to say. It's often the case that lovers want to help each other. But Wood can perceive such "help" as criticism, causing friction in the relationship.

When Wood is frustrated with work or some other challenge in the outer world, their romantic partner can make all the difference. Intimacy, laughter, and sharing in a tender way can turn it right around for them. With that level of connection with their loved one, they can get right back up on their horse and ride out, head held high, smile on their face.

Are You in Love with Wood?

Is your partner Wood? Watch how your Wood lover interacts with the world, through the eyes, the walk, and the sound of the voice.

The Walk: Ten Feet Tall in a Six-Foot Town

It doesn't matter how tall or short they are, Woods just look big. Think Napoleon big in a small package. The reason they turn heads when they walk into a room isn't just that they think they're something special (which they often do), but also because of how they hold the energy in their bodies. Remember, it's all about energy in this world.

Wood energy is centered in the diaphragm area below the chest. They puff out this area to create a look of being bigger than average. It's as if they propel themselves forward in life from that area of their upper abdomen, between their ribs. They do this unconsciously, as we are all unaware of how we hold our energy in our bodies.

When they walk, they look as if they're penguins on parade. They puff out their diaphragms, and their elbows come out a bit. They somewhat resemble toy soldiers, and their legs step out without bending the knee and their feet land heavily. They love to wear big shoes to emphasize this fact. A heavy walk creates an air of strength, and they love to be perceived as strong. Note: While penguins do have feet, they do not wear heavy shoes.

You might also notice in bed that your lover is very muscular, even if they are not working out. The Wood element is about strength and athletic prowess, so it's as if they don't even have to try to work out to have awesome muscle definition.

The Talk: Do What I Want Now (Please)

Wood gives orders. Oh, they're very nice about it. They'll often add "please" or "thank you" at the end of a sentence. But if you listen to their sentence structure, they mostly speak in commands. However, many of them have developed qualities that make it easy for people to do what they ask without feeling put out. Not all Woods have mastered this art (some can be quite gruff or even rude), but many have found ways to make this natural delegation work for them. In fact, some are so skilled at it, they make you think they're doing you a favor when you do their bidding! Like a modern-day Tom Sawyer, some Woods seemingly glide through life with a team of people who love to help them along the journey. Wood loves win-win in all areas, all the time.

Most of us are totally unaware of how Woods do this. It's all in subtle behaviors, like the natural sound of their voice, which can make even a disobedient dog sit every time. What makes it so effective? Woods speak in short, truncated phrases, sometimes not even full sentences. By having short choppy phrases, Woods can emphasize the words that are important so that the listener is really clear about what they want.

If you ask Woods a question, they'll usually find the shortest phrase as a reply that answers the question. For example, if you ask them how they got here today, they might give you a two-word answer, such as, "By car." If you ask another Elemental type like Fire how they got here, you might get a story about the entire journey to the place, including where they stopped for coffee.

Wood even tends to break up longer words into shortened syllables, as if the words are just too long to speak. Think "super-cali-fragi-listic-expe-ali-docious" spoken in chopped up syllables instead of one word. This breaking up of syllables makes the speech seem even more direct and to the point.

They also speak in an even tone, without the variety of high and low notes that other elements have. Instead of the voice going up and down for emphasis, Wood uses the strength of the voice to make you listen. You can hear the force of consonants, like the p's, k's, and t's, literally pop out of their mouths like bullets firing.

They also sound like they're shouting even when they're not. But remember Wood loves to be funny and laugh. So despite the monotone sounding voice, they're very engaged and animated in life. They are constantly testing you to see if you're awake. They'll throw out a quip and see how fast you can have a comeback. A five-second response time is slow for them. Seconds are eons in Wood time.

In their quieter moments, however, Wood can be quite gentle and soft, even in their speech. The monotone will still be there, but there is much more tenderness when they're in a peaceful state.

The Look: Wood-Boring Eyes into Your Soul

When Woods smile, which is often, it's as if the smile doesn't extend up to their eyes. Sometimes the eyes look cold, like shark eyes, making some people uncomfortable. But don't mistake the lack of warmth in the eyes for being unloving. On the contrary, Woods are fun-loving friends and playmates.

Like a puppy's, Wood eyes are seemingly asking the world, do you want to play? If they had a tail, they would wag it when they met someone who looks friendly or interesting. It's all in their eyes. They bore into you unwaveringly, hoping you'll want to engage. Many people can't hold Wood's gaze and have to look away.

What Does Wood Want— The Bigger the Better

If you're Wood, you want a partner who makes you feel big and is totally, utterly *into you*. You're looking for a partner who sees the greatness in you. Your lover has to see all the amazing qualities of you and see the incredible deeds you can perform. If your lover is not paying attention in a big way to all you do, it's not going to happen for you. You're like a little kid up on the stone wall, standing on one foot while balancing a ball on your head, asking over and over, "Mom, watch me!" Were you that kid? Even if you want to deny it, you know it's true!

Yet when your partner sees you, you don't need a lot of praise at all. A quick acknowledgement is enough...a high five, thumbs up, a big kiss will do. These gestures say, "Yes, I'm watching you; you're awesome!" It's the best reward for a job well done. It's what Wood lives for.

Even if you have the self-confidence to be your own cheering section, it sure feels good to have someone else to cheer you on. Besides that fact, you do want someone who can engage you very actively. Engaging requires a level of participation that some people don't want to give or are incapable of giving.

Some people prefer to live life in a more floaty way (see chapter six) that is disengaged with the world. The Earth element engages deeply on the mental level through in-depth, thoughtful conversation. While this is a valid type of engagement, it can be too heady for most Wood types. Wood likes engagement that's fun, not a lot of emotional conversation and drama. More action, more doing, like, "Hey, let's play a fun game" or throwing down the gauntlet of a new challenge.

So if you're Wood, you're looking for a romantic partner who is fundamentally easy to have fun with and who shares your sense of humor. You want to be going places, accomplishing things, and playing games—living life to the fullest and having a blast doing it (in a fair, safe, honest, and compassionate yet motivating way). You have to be on the same team as Wood. You want your partner to be a co-captain on your team with equal say, even though you're likely to be giving all the orders. That is the Wood way—simple yet complicated.

The Evolution of Wood

If you're Wood, you don't really want to admit you need accolades for all you do. Ultimately any of the Five Elements wants to be able to give themselves what they want and not need it from a romantic partner. Self-sufficiency makes for much healthier relationships.

The evolution of the Wood element is to see their own greatness and to engage themselves on a high, spiritual level. When Wood isn't looking externally for stimulation or challenges, they can begin to search for their inner peace. They can become selflessly awesome. In the Chinese classical texts, the image for the evolved Wood is the warrior come back from well-fought lifelong battles to contemplate in the garden. Peace at last.

March forward, Wood, and be great!

Four

Fire—
Light My Fire

....

"But enough about me. Let's talk about you.
What do you think of me?"
CC Bloom (Bette Midler) in "Beaches"

....

Everyone loves them. People love to help them. They're fun, joyful, and full of laughter. They love to make everyone happy. Fire is the life of the party in the Elemental world. Yes, if Fire ruled the world, it would be one big party! Whoopee! Let the balloons fly, and pop the corks on the endless champagne bottles. If only life were that easy.

Fire People Have it Easy, Right?

Although it rarely happens, Fires, unlike Woods, are delighted when they arrive on time to a party. Mostly they'll show up late due to wardrobe and GPS malfunctions. However, they're likely the last to go home (unless the party moves to a more intimate or romantic location early!). It's all about parties, social situations, and sweet love with you Fire peeps.

Life is focused on people. Fires may walk into room full of people and not notice that the room's decor has been completely changed since the last visit simply because they're exerting all their energy trying to see who's at the party.

Fire is designed for love. Not just etheric love, but hot, sexual love. They smolder with sex and sexuality. They dress to entice those around them into thinking about it. They are masters at seduction and are irresistible to those who interact with them. Many Fires think about sex in every conversation, and often turn the topic to naughty innuendoes—not dirty-minded, but just risqué enough to make everyone laugh nervously. They just love a conversation with a sexual edge. In fact, what else is there to talk about REALLY, but love, sex, or, even better … falling in love and then having sex. Love makes the world go round, and Fires are the agents of love.

Are Your Fires Burning?

It feels wonderful to be joyful and happy with people. But mean people can completely thwart Fire's outgoing-ness. "MEAN PEOPLE SUCK" could very well be Fire's bumper sticker, stuck on the back of their hearts. The more open-hearted Fire wants to be, the more protected and cautious they are in situations that feel unsafe. Good thing Fires are made out of rubber and bounce back like no other Element. As soon as they're back on track, they revert back to their wonderful, sexy ways.

Fire doesn't always recognize themselves in the descriptions above because they think of themselves as quite shy. However, with people they know, they are gregarious, easy, and fun loving. It's just strangers who make them feel vulnerable. The meanness factor is their big challenge. Meanness has so many layers, and it's everywhere in our society. Fires have to overcome the cruelty of the world and put themselves out there over and over ... and over again despite the potential consequences.

Celebrities Who Sizzle!

The world is filled with hot sexy Fire types who light it up all the time! Big Hollywood actors like Leonardo DiCaprio and Orlando Bloom are red-hot Fire. Amy Adams, Anne Hathaway, and Drew Barrymore are all sexy but vulnerable Fire stars who twinkle on the big screen. Pop superstars Justin Bieber and Usher are sexy Fire men who burn up the stages. Elton John rocks as well as Adam Levine of Maroon 5 (both Fire). Freddie Mercury and Janis Joplin were bright sparks of Fire in their times, totally wearing their hearts out on their sleeves for all the world to see.

It doesn't stop there when it comes to Fire superstars in the world. Let's not forget the legendary actresses and co-medians Lily Tomlin, Shirley MacLaine, and Bette Midler. Super sexy mega-athletes like Tom Brady and David Beckham (whose wives Gisele Bündchen and Victoria Beckham are, interestingly, both strong Wood) compete on the field, showing off their sexy athletic skills and hot bods.

Smarties with Heart

Fire's power of persuasion is very useful in business and politics as well. Some amazing business people are strong Fires, whose formula for success is their mixture of business smarts with the power of persuasion. Sheryl Sandberg of Facebook and Meg Whitman of eBay and Hewlett-Packard are in the forefront of Fire business women. Business mogul and adventurer Richard Branson of the Virgin empire is the epitome of a successful Fire business person. Branson didn't listen to naysayers—he passionately pursued what his heart told him people wanted even when the bankers refused to back the creation of his airline.

Fires make excellent salespeople because they *understand what people desire.* They can *feel* what's the best thing to say to convince someone of anything. Their enthusiasm is compelling and contagious. But as people-pleasers, they might say one thing to one person and then something completely different to another but are totally sincere to each.

The power of politics and its access to large audiences also attracts Fires, like former U.S. President Bill Clinton. He was the master of making people feel included in his conversations, having "Town Hall" meetings with regular voters, warming them with laughter and stories. He always sought common ground. His charismatic ways went far with people, but his romantic interests did not.

Firespeak to Me

Fires are also great communicators, writers, teachers, and storytellers. They love to talk, so they usually choose a vocation that involves doing a lot of communicating, spoken or written.

Fires feel, but do they actually listen? You'd think a strong communicator would be a great listener, but not so for Fire. Fire has difficulty listening to what others are saying, often because Fire is thinking about what to say next. It's very hard for them to wait for you to finish a sentence because they don't want to lose track of their thoughts.

When two Fires are talking, they jump in and interrupt, finishing each other's sentences back and forth. The excitement builds and builds as they talk. Fires expect these interruptions and don't mind being interrupted. In fact, they like it because they enjoy sharing the dialogue completely. They are feeling the emotions of the conversation and enjoy the fun and excitement of exchanging words, thoughts, and emotions.

When Fires do listen, they're listening to the *emotion* of what you're saying rather than the words. For example, if you're unhappy and trying to hide it, they'll sense your true mood and call you out. They may be a bit sketchy about remembering *what* you said but they know *how* you feel. Sometimes partners of Fire can become quite frustrated at what they think is inattention even if they're intently listening for something else—what your heart is saying.

Really, for Fire the point of talking at all is to open hearts and connect. They make their lovers feel safe with their smile and warmth. They appear to be listening intently in order to sense the emotions behind the words. They may ask you leading questions that evoke emotions, and they're always working to find the way for you to let down your guard and explore deeper and further. Some people might be slightly uncomfortable with their disarming questions. Others don't seem to mind at all.

Once you open your heart and connect with them, Fires fall in love. They're all yours. They can be openhearted with you all day long. That's when it gets good for Fire. A heart connection with someone they are totally into makes Fire feel complete.

Since it's all about making that connection, it's hard for them to talk about things they're not interested in. How can you have an openhearted discussion if you aren't talking about something you're both passionate about? It can be quite annoying when you realize they're often changing the topic to find something you're both interested in.

Me, Myself, and Fire

If they can't connect with someone, they get very nervous and talkative, filling in gaps in the conversation with seemingly needless chatter. They'll ask a question, and before you get a chance to answer, they offer various options like a multiple-choice quiz. Here is a fun way to have fun with Fire. Anyone with a poker face drives them crazy! They can't know what you're thinking.

Don't answer their question and see what happens. "What do you take in your coffee?" they ask. Pause…wait for it…it only takes about a second…"Sugar? Milk? Maybe two sugars?" Uh-oh, more silence, as they start to unravel…"Do you like it black, then?" "Yes?" "You know what? I can just bring it all! Do you even like sugar? I like sugar."

They've even been accused of only thinking about themselves. What, those fun-loving Fires? Vain? Narcissistic? Well, maybe a little, but with loving (and sexy) intentions perhaps. In fact, they really want their loved ones to be happy. But they'll often ask you if you're happy with them, which is why other people think in the end, it's still all about them!

Rebel Without a Pause

Fires are the true rebels in the Elemental world. In every sense of the word, they emblazon paths that might send others scurrying back to the norm of the society. They're your classic early adopters of new things…new technology, new fashion, new ideas. They love to shock people with outlandish, new, but smart thoughts. They use knowledge as a tool for standing out in the world. Don't tell Fire they can't do something that's new and exciting. That will ensure they'll do it!

In fact, they might be doing a lot of new and exciting things at once. The problem is, how does one focus on any one thing? There are shiny temptations everywhere, and they are drawn to them like moths to a flame. Maybe they need a business coach to get them focused, preferably the Wood Element type.

Silver Lining in Every Cloud

When life is about love and joy, why do people insist on being so serious, mean, and just no fun? This is the quandary of Fire's life. They are full of optimism. In the way that Wood refuses to follow rules and think inside the box, Fire finds the silver lining in every cloud, and then they sprinkle happy thoughts all over it.

They may not be able to solve the world's problems, but they can help almost anyone find the brighter side to anything. They lift people up with their positivity—a real Fire word. People love to come and bask in the glow of their firelight. Fire doesn't believe that anything in the world is worth being depressed over for long. Even at a funeral, they may feel compelled to tell funny stories or little jokes to lift peoples' moods.

Six Degrees of Non-separation

Fire loves to inspire other people about things they feel passionate about. A strong Fire cannot only convince one or two friends to do anything; they can convince fifty people to do something really wild!

Fire is never short on friends. Some Fires believe they only have a small circle of close friends. Ha! That's funny. Most of them have many people in their lives that really want to be their friends! And those friends have even more friends who want to meet this inspiring Fire. Without Fire, who'd initiate the many social activities in the world today? Get one Fire to join, and their admirers will join too!

Pollyanna Want a Cracker?

What does Fire really want from a relationship? What's going to really make Fire's soul sing? If you are Fire, it's someone who's totally and passionately in love with you.

Fire is about attraction—being attracted to someone or being attractive to others. Fire wants to find that communion with another where the sparks begin to fly. Fires want to be ignited or ignite someone else with their passion. You might think that the passion in a relationship fades after the honeymoon is over, but many Fire couples maintain the same excitement with each other for years and years. Sure, relationships mature and change, but it's the original connection that matters and ultimately lasts. It's an enthusiasm and excitement to share life together that secures that heart connection for Fire.

The organ associated with Fire is the heart. Remember we talked about the heart as the "circulation sex official" in the second chapter? The heart is in charge of our ability to feel turned on. It's that almost electric feeling that some call passion or lust, in which your whole body feels like it's suddenly on fire. It's why we say, "I'm burning for you." How do you think the word "hot" began to mean "sexy"? It must have come from Fire, who was literally burning for a lover!

This is about the little love tendrils that come out of your heart and bring life force energy to every part of your body, like being plugged into a light socket. We call this the Network of Animation, or the *mai* in Chinese Medicine. It's the network of your life force. When you're attracted to something, this network is activated, and you become "on fire," making you feel alive and passionate.

Windows to the Sexy Soul

Sex with Fire is a tumbling swirl of passion. It's always changing and always performed with gusto. But most of all, it's the meeting of two individuals feeling a heart connection. That heart connection creates passion in both people simultaneously.

Alternating between sweet and soft, and wild and untamed, Fire sex constantly changes tempo. Think of a campfire burning from its quiet coals to a raging bonfire. One minute you might be filled with lust, and the next minute, quiet and attentive. The number one factor is changeability. Sameness is deadly and kills the attraction for Fire.

Fires can get bored if they feel their partner slowing down and losing the connection. They need that passion to be ignited at all times. So if you're the type of person who is slow and sensual in bed, you might lose your Fire playmate, who needs to feel your attention, excitement, and attraction at all times. Fire needs things to be changed up a lot so as to reignite the passion in each moment. They need some affirmation of your continued attraction and excitement over and over.

Fires also need to connect often through the eyes, those windows to the soul. But for Fires, these windows open straight through the heart. Fires use the eyes to make very intense heart connections. When they can see your eyes, they can feel how passionate (or not) you are in the moment.

Spark Plugs at Full Spark

Cold, hard sex will not satisfy Fire for long. What really heats up Fire is when their lover is attracted to them. So, they may try to be as seductive as possible. If they can light a spark in you, then their Fire gets stoked! Their passion gets ignited, and then it fuels more fire in you. It just builds and builds, like a fire with the right kind of fuel, getting hotter and hotter.

But for Fire, that only happens if the spark is there. If Fire isn't physically attracted to you, not much will happen. Their heart may be closed. Someone who can potentially be a passionate fireball with the right partner might feel as cold as ice with another person. When a Fire's heart closes, it's like hell just froze over. They can be cold and seemingly unfeeling to someone from whom they feel disconnected.

Throwing a Bucket
of Water on the Fire

Nothing rings the death knell on a relationship with Fire more than partners stating they are no longer attracted to the person. Unfortunately, Fires get so excited about life that sometimes they forget to attend to their looks. Then they might start to feel bad about their body, and their partner might make a comment or drop a hint about their looks, outfit, or general appearance. That spells derailment for Fire. They melt down like butter on a Florida highway. It's an instant image crisis.

When couples go through this, we suggest that both parties attend to their bodies. They need to create a focused environment to do whatever it takes for Fire to feel and look good again. Of course, Fire is beautiful no matter what the outer body looks like because they emit an inner beauty. This inner beauty is only dimmed when Fire's self-image suffers. And when they don't feel good inside, they lose their sex drive. One Fire we know lost his desire to have sex after losing his hair and gaining weight. He felt bad about his body image and stopped having sex with his wife, even though he still loved her and had enjoyed sex before that time. He never told her why, and the situation lasted years before they finally discussed the reason for the problem.

The Laughing Heart

Laughter is one of the ways Fires like to share in love. Laughter opens the heart and encourages closer connections. The more laughter and lovemaking, the better!

Fires are flirtatious. Unless they rein themselves in or shut their bright light in a box, people are always going to be attracted to them. It can be difficult to have a monogamous relationship with Fires who are easily distracted by other interesting people. The relationship has to be really solid to prevent Fire from looking elsewhere. As long as they feel very fulfilled in the love department, then they are steadfast and satisfied.

Fires can also look for someone who makes them feel safe, someone who loves their faults as much as their gifts, and someone with whom who they can be completely authentic. They might make comments about negative aspects of their body or personality. Often they want to expose the negative parts of themselves and ask, "Do you still love me?"

It's all about unconditional love. They know better than anyone that they're not perfect. They don't expect you to be perfect either. But they also know everyone deserves love. So they are extremely forgiving. They will love your faults as well as your gifts. You might have hurt them unwittingly (or even wittingly), but if you're still willing to love them, they will come round and love you back.

Because they think everyone has imperfections, you might be surprised if your Fire lover wants to talk about your faults a lot. They might want to have discussions about the things they think you're screwing up. Especially if you're Wood, you might not want to dwell on your negative attributes. This desire to often discuss imperfections could be a challenge in some relationships.

Open and Shut Case

When Fire's feelings get hurt, they can feel disconnected, which brings the relationship to a grinding halt. Fires certainly can't make love feeling this way (unless they're faking it and just going through the motions). When this happens, they often feel an obsessive need to resolve the problem through talking about the same issues over and over.

They may frantically try to find a way back to connection. Communication is the only answer to a closed heart for them. It's intolerable to feel any disconnection from their lover's heart. They'd rather hash it out and find common ground as soon as possible to alleviate the pain of disagreement.

After quite a bit of conversation, Fire can feel safe again. Whenever Fire's heart reopens after having been slammed shut, tears often come. This is usually a good thing because it's almost past. Fire feels immediately better after disclosing their inner feelings and crying. For Fire, it's about *feeling* the openness of the other person's heart. It's that simple really.

But the second that the partner's heart closes again, the panic sets in with Fire desperately searching for a way back in. The partner can easily reassure Fire with statements like this:

"This isn't about you," or "We're okay. I'm just upset about this other thing, and I'd like to talk to you about it tonight."

Turning the Other Cheek

Sometimes Fires take their forgiving attitude a bit too far. They might be more likely to put up with an abusive partner when they keep focusing that person's good parts, especially if the abuse is mild. They'll make excuses to their friends, stating the good qualities over and over as if they've made a balance sheet of good and bad qualities. As long as the good outweighs the bad and they really love the person, they'll endure a great deal.

So, Fires have a tendency to get into codependent relationships because they have difficulty expressing their true feelings. Then a level of inauthenticity can creep in. That's when Fire has feelings about something, and they're covering them up either consciously or unconsciously. They may lose themselves entirely in the relationship.

The Crying Game

The only thing worth crying about is, of course, *love*! New love, deep love, or lost love.

When Fire loses love, a grand melodrama of enormous proportions follows. Every time. If you live for love, but love deserts you, well, life just doesn't feel worth living. The "woe is me" lament flares up. And everyone around you is going to hear about it!

A Fire's life is always up and down, like the flames of a fire. They can't always be brilliant and full of joy. Sometimes they come down and feel sad for a bit. But not for long! They recover and move on. There's always something else to feel happy about somewhere in the world. They can't help it! Fire will always find a new person to love.

Beep … Beep … Beep

When life is good for Fire, they don't feel the need to constantly protect themselves from the harsh world. They can maintain a state of contentment and joy, with a gentle bouncing along, with mild ups and downs, like a heart-rate monitor. One thing's for sure … Fire avoids flatness at any level. Even too much joy sustained for too long isn't good. No one can sustain constant laughter, for example. But an emotional flatline will only occur the day that a Fire dies. Until then, Fire must always go up and down.

For this reason, sometimes Fires are accused of being moody, especially when they have been hurt a lot. They're always on the lookout for meanness all around them. They might even accuse you of being mean when you weren't trying to be! As a result, people might accuse Fire of being manic/depressive, even though a psychiatrist wouldn't diagnose them that way. It's just that their natural up and down nature occasionally goes into overdrive due to fear or loneliness.

When Fire has to resort to living this way, so protected, so shut down from love, it's sad. They can't shine their inner light when they feel it's unsafe to open their hearts. Then others may suffer too because Fire can themselves be mean when their hearts are closed. They don't like to be mean to anyone, but every now and then they can't help it.

Chinese philosophers believed the path of Fire is to learn how to live openhearted and unprotected all the time. They say the best protection is no protection. This means that if someone is mean, Fire needs to see that it's the other person's pain and problem, not their own.

Strip Poker—A Game of Words

Watching two Fires talk together is like watching two people play verbal strip poker. The first person will tease or playfully taunt the other about some aspect of themselves. The second person will laugh nervously, play along, admit it's true, and come back with an equally targeted tease, disarming the other player a bit, in a fun and playful way. The first round is over. Now comes the next round. They go back and forth, and so on.

It's a playful banter in a very serious game of making each other vulnerable. The hidden question behind the conversation could be: Will you be true and show me your imperfections? Can you laugh at yourself and help me laugh at myself? Together being vulnerable helps us connect. That's how it works. Fire wants to create more access to your heart.

They think that vulnerability allows one to be more open and exposed.

When both partners can be open to each other without being mean-spirited, Fire feels very safe and present. They no longer need to hide all those imperfections and can be authentic.

Fires avoid people who are mad or angry with them. Sometimes they're overly sensitive, misperceiving anger when it really isn't there. On occasion, they may even withhold the truth or lie to avoid provoking their lover's anger, resulting in inauthenticity. As the relationship matures, it may appear like Fire is being a little secretive, and they are. They're trying to please you and make everything feel better.

Simply BE Love

When Fire falls in love, they can lose themselves in the other person, which opens up a host of challenges. For example, they may sacrifice their own needs and do whatever their partner wants in order to be reassured that they are loved. While love is their first priority, Fire has to follow what makes them feel passionate about life. If they subjugate that to make their romantic partner happy, then their health often suffers. They need to speak up about their passion for life and love.

One Fire told us that he'd ignored his passion for art in order to support his wife and children. His sacrifice led to severe health issues and almost ended his marriage. In a last ditch effort to save the relationship, the couple went to counseling together. His wife didn't even know his true feelings. Once they identified that he'd given up his art for his family commitments, the relationship began to improve. In time, he found a healthy balance that allowed him to enjoy both successfully.

The truth is that the world wants Fire to pursue their many passions because that's what's so exciting about Fire— their passion! Hiding their true feelings always ends up in disappointment and disillusionment. Once Fires realize they get to have fun *and* be in love, they're awesome partners. Being true to themselves is the ultimate goal, thus allowing people to love them for who they truly are.

Are You in Love with Fire?

Fire is upbeat and makes you want to smile and laugh. But how can you tell if your partner is Fire? You can observe how your lover interacts with the world, through the eyes, the walk, and the sound of the voice. The way people move tells you about their Elemental Energy type.

First, watch their body—a fun way to start. Where does your partner hold energy in their body? For Fire, it is centered in the chest from the heart up, and looks like everything is lifting up on the person's body. Think of it like they have champagne in their body and the effervescent, giggly bubbles are trying to burst up and out.

The Walk: Rising to the Occasion

When Fires walk, it's almost like there's helium in their shoulders trying to lift them off the ground. They literally bounce when they walk! Their heels come off the ground and propel them up and down. Some appear to be walking on their toes.

This upward movement is also noticeable in their faces. They actually lift their eyebrows when they speak. And of course that sexy, friendly smile is always there.

Unlike Woods, who have a goal-oriented walk (they pick a point and find the fastest way there), Fires are easily distracted from getting to their destination. They might even completely forget where they were originally going if they encounter a friend along the way. They can get distracted and easily diverted by things that catch their eye. We say Fire is "shiny," meaning they are attracted to attractive things. They like colors and bling. Distractions shift their attention. You might send them to the store for eggs, and find they come back with a grocery bag full of interesting things to show you, but no eggs! Then in a high voice, they might laughingly exclaim, "Oopsy!" They hope you'll laugh with them at their little shopping faux pas.

The Talk: Tiny Bubbles

Not only do they bounce when they walk, but their voices bounce! It's as if those champagne bubbles are now making the Fire voice bubble up into a happy, upbeat, excited voice. Their voices go up and down and are the most varied of all the Elements. Water can have some sudden dramatic flares in the sound of their voice, but mostly they are monotone (see chapter seven). The Fire voice goes up and down, like sharp peaks and valleys. It's not a sing-songy voice (see chapter five) that smoothly goes up and down lyrically.

Fire has a voice that connotes excitement. It reaches out to your ears and tickles them with high tones so that you want to hear. The voice sounds thrilling, even if they're talking about something boring. They're often the best storytellers because they hold your interest. Often it seems like they might break into laughter at any moment, even when they're trying to be serious.

Then there's the sexy smoldering voice of Fire. They have this ability to assume a very sexy voice that entices those who are attracted to them. The sound can be throaty and full of promise of what's to come. Even this sexy voice has that up-and-down quality, though more sultry. Fire's voice seems to be suggesting something more, though shyness often gets in the way of delivering on that promise.

The Look: Twinkle, Twinkle Little Fire Star

The voice and walk show the upward lifting movement for Fire. But the eyes are the biggest giveaway—Fire eyes twinkle. Yes, it's true; they can't help it. Their bright light shines from their eyes. It's like seeing twinkling little stars peeking out. When they smile, their eyes smile with them.

They have flirty eyes too. They look at you, look away all coy and shy…and then look back again. Their eyes are seemingly asking the question, "Do you like me?" The more smiley and safe you look to them, the more comfortable they are with you, and the more they can look at you directly.

In love relationships, Fires communicate through their eyes. Fires want to see what's really inside you. They need to see your eyes while making love to get a sense of what you're feeling.

What Does Fire Want— Love Me, No Matter What

Fires want their partner to pay attention and be attracted to them, despite any perceived flaws. They might even point out their flaws to you, especially in bed, which is a bit of a turn off for Wood, who only wants to look at you in the best way possible.

It's simple. They want unconditional love. Fire wants you to be aware of the fact that they have more good features than bad. They don't want to cover up the bad ... just celebrate the good.

The Evolution of Fire

Ultimately, the evolutionary path for Fire's growth lies in realizing that your best lover and best friend is truly your own self. People are going to love you passionately, but over time these relationships may wane. Others may last a lifetime. But if you rely on any person to give you love because you don't love yourself, you will struggle find inner happiness. You will always be afraid of losing that love.

Once you fall in love with yourself, you can embark on your true destiny, which is to share your love and light with everyone else.

Go forth, Fire, and love thyself!

Five

Earth—
Love Sherpa

....

"It's not how much we give but
how much love we put into giving."
Mother Teresa

....

What makes the world go round? Earth. Without you, the Earth people, nothing would get done. The rest of us don't realize that our world is built on your Earth backbone. You are amazingly hard workers. It's not that the rest of us aren't doing anything, but for sure we're not doing as much as you, if you are indeed Earth. And we're certainly not being as thorough.

Workhorse that you are, you are so much more. You are a caring, sensual, alluring person who envelops your loved ones in sweet, soft goodness. You give and give, and the rest of the world takes and takes and takes, often without any gratitude. But you? You don't stop giving just because they're taking. You take in nourishment from the land, air, and water. You transform these ingredients into even more giving-ness, like a tree that bears fruit for all to enjoy.

Earth's beauty is the girl-next-door kind. At home, day-to-day, they're down to earth. They love to wear jeans and a comfy t-shirt. But give them a reason to dress up, and they're all about looking good and sexy. There are different kinds of sexy. Wood's sexy appeal is charismatic and sporty. Fire has a bling-bling, passionate sexiness. Now we've got sensual, smooth, delicious Earth sexy. It's the kind of sexy that makes you go, "mmmm-mmmm good."

This makes sense since Earth is all about food—making food, eating food, appreciating food, and giving food to family and friends. For Earth, the body becomes something to share, like food. It's like an innocent and pure sensuality—simple and luscious, fleshy and enticing.

Earth Girls (and Boys) Are Not Easy

Despite the 1980s movie title *Earth Girls Are Easy*, Earth girls (and boys for that matter) are NOT easy.

If you're Earth, you might make it look easy and have everyone around you fooled. But your life is far from easy because you care so much about everyone else.

Give and No Take

Does everyone around you depend on all the things you do, maybe even taking you for granted because you make it look so easy? Are you a person who invests so much of yourself into your relationships with your lovers, parents, children, friends, and coworkers? Do you like to take your time even when people are trying to rush you? Do you like to think things through, analyze all your options carefully, and plan accordingly before you make a move? Are you the kind of person who actually reads all those instruction manuals? You know, the ones you keep in the baggies in the kitchen junk drawer.

If you are resonating with these questions, you need to consider that you are likely Earth (or have Earth second in your Elemental Energetic type).

Earth loves to play supporting roles for their children, families, parents, and coworkers. Even the jobs they pick are often supporting roles. Many psychologists, teachers, and hospitality managers are Earth. They are people who like to help. When we did a workshop for a large hair salon recently, 95 percent of the hair stylists were Earth. The only non-Earth employees in the group were the owners (who were Wood and Fire). People ask for Earth hair stylists because they really listen and intuitively sense what you really want in a hairstyle. They're multi-talented, really give attention to your problems, help you find solutions if you ask, and give you a good haircut that matches the picture you had in your mind. Let's see your therapist do that!

Earth's Most Powerful Man

Although supportive by nature, Earths can also be major leaders. U.S. President Barack Obama showed the world that an Earth can be at the top. But he didn't do it alone—he came to power at a time when the country was in trouble and needed the type of person who was going to analyze and consider all possible outcomes. He built a whole support system to solve the country's challenges. He had a strong Wood partner, his wife Michelle, as a source of strength to back him.

Earths are particularly suited to lead companies that may need a lot of consensus and community building. Anne Sweeney is one such powerful Earth leader at Disney Media Networks. This style of leadership is more caring-based, not to be confused with weakness. It's strong on values and being supportive.

Hollywood's Earthly A-List

Musical Earth superstar Beyoncé Knowles's rise to the top was built on hard work and dedication. Earth is never afraid of hard work. But she's not doing it alone either. She's built a dedicated support team. She also supports women musicians, inviting the best from around the world to join her on stage when she tours the globe.

Jennifer Aniston is Hollywood's quintessential Earth girl next door. She's worked her Earthly talents into many Hollywood blockbusters. But her big break in her career was on the TV show *Friends* as the character Rachel. How fitting that an Earth woman rises to stardom with her friends at her side!

Another Earth woman who has benefitted from an ensemble TV cast on *Saturday Night Live* is Kristin Wiig. This talented comedian and writer went on to appear in the hit movie *Bridesmaids*. *The Voice's* Christina Aguilera sings her amazing vocals and struts her sexy Earth moves on music stages worldwide. She, like Beyoncé, also supports empowering women.

The Element that Keeps on Giving... and Giving

If you're Earth, you're born to give. Giving is your gift to the world. A gift is more than just a physical object you buy for someone. Earth giving involves incredible thoughtfulness. For example, some people (especially impatient Fire) might think buying a birthday gift is as simple as running into the store at the last minute and asking the salesperson to help you find something interesting. That would never fly if you're Earth. Earth might wonder, "What's meaningful about selecting something that would be suitable for just anyone?" No, you need to find the perfect gift based on what you know about the person.

Not only do you want to find a gift the recipient will like, but you also want to find a gift that shows that person that you truly understand their wishes, needs, or interests. A gift often involves making something especially for the recipient, selecting a special poem, creating a card, or perhaps bringing small tokens with significant meanings. It's not important how expensive the gift is but how personal and thoughtful it is.

Want to make an Earth's birthday special? Organize a party that not only celebrates but also honors that person. Ask guests to share their gratitude for that person's values and efforts. Earth has organized these parties countless times for others and will be incredibly touched by the effort you put into the party. One woman who has planned dozens of such parties over many years lamented that no one ever plans parties for her because she does it so well.

Earth knows that giving a gift is an act of love and caring. You give away something of yourself. In order to give like this, you have to have something to give. For Earth, this means you have to receive first and foremost.

The Fruits of Your Labor

In nature, a fruit tree receives the sun and rain during spring and summer so it can produce the fruits of its labor in autumn. So it's imperative that Earths attend to themselves daily and be open to receiving what others give them.

What is nourishment really? On the literal level, it's food. But it's also taking a warm bath, meditating, doing yoga, getting a manicure, or going to therapy; even sexual satisfaction might be a self-care issue in some people's lives. Earths take time for themselves when they need to. The self-help book industry was built for them! Self-care is receiving without feeling guilty. It's also about not relying on anyone else to give to you.

Once they take in their daily dose of nourishment, receiving something good, they then have to get back to what they do best . . . giving. The stomach is Earth's organ, and its job is to receive nourishment, mash it all up, and give it away to the rest of the body. If it doesn't give all that goodness away, it ends up bloated and unable to go to the bathroom! That's not good. Earths who get resentful and stop giving are metaphorically constipated. So it's important to keep on giving no matter what so you don't get backed up.

BFFs

As Earth, you're looking for a lover who is emotionally accessible. People who hold back or hide a part of themselves are not candidates. You give everything of yourself to your loved-ones. You want to feel your loved one's presence and merge with them. And most importantly, you want a companion and a best friend, someone with whom to share your life.

Loving Taskmaster

Sensuality is part of Earth. In comparison, Metal (discussed in the next chapter) has a heightened tactile sense. Metal enjoys sex as a sensual experience, whereas Earths use their senses to get in tune with a lover. The average person has five senses, right? Well, Earth is so sensitive, it's like they have ten. It's about being able to sense what your lover wants or needs in bed, almost as if they're reading your mind. Wow—they already sensed what you want before you even knew it!

Bonding or Bondage?

Because Earth already knows what you like, they have no problem being in charge. But their leadership is different than Wood's bossy-pants assertiveness. They don't tell you what to do; they just do it. They can get on top and drive. They do this sweetly, of course; they're Earth. But they want you to let go and trust them. They know what they're doing and do it well; so just let them do their thing. Afterwards, they would like you to take over at some point and give back to them.

Let's put it this way: If you want a strong lover who works hard, find an Earth person. They can feel into you, know you deeply, understand you, and really get you. This kind of loving isn't for the faint of heart. Earth is slow, and they love a process. Sex is just another process—it has a beginning, middle, and an end. It's a passage through time, a journey. It's at times tender and sensual. But it can also be very strong and powerful.

Just a word of caution, Earth will dominate you if you let them, both in and outside the bedroom. Now that's not a bad thing in itself, it's just the way it is. One strong Fire said being with his Earth wife made him feel weak and that he needed to be stronger to meet her equally. She challenged him sexually, which he liked, once he felt safe and learned how to really meet her.

Playing All the Instruments

Remember we said that Earth girls (and boys) aren't easy? Well, there is a price for such an awesome lover. The price is that you can't be asleep at the wheel. You have to pay attention. Earths must be nurtured and doing well in themselves before they are able to give as much as they do.

If you have been disinterested, uninvolved, and not listening—basically holding out on your Earth lover emotionally, the first thing they will do is hold out on you sexually. They simply cannot give to you in *that* way when you've been inconsiderate and unhelpful to them. They can't feel into you if they perceive you as shut down. And they certainly can't make love when they're resentful and themselves shut down. Sex after an argument as a way to kiss and make up is probably *not* going to happen too often.

Earths believe that making love has to come from a place of understanding. If there's a problem in a relationship, nothing fun is going to happen that night until a lot of *talking* occurs first. They have to get to the bottom of an argument and find a harmony before they can open up again.

In fact, think of it as more than opening up. Really what Earth needs is to merge totally with you. They become one with you through sex. In that merging, it's as if the two of you are one organism moving in unison. It's like in an orchestra playing the most beautiful harmonic music. You might flatter yourself that you play an amazing first violin, but your Earth partner plays, oh let's see … *all the remaining instruments* in the orchestra expertly and in perfect pitch. As usual, they make it look easy.

Love Sherpa

If you're Earth, you will often carry a much heavier load than your non-Earth partner. You do the majority of the hard work in the relationship because you are very capable of it, and it makes you feel wanted and useful. Oh, and the other reason you do it, is, ahem, you're so much *better* at it. We're talking housework, bills, shopping, social engagements…let's face it, your partner can try to help, but when they're not looking, you might have to reload that dishwasher or mop that floor again because they missed a ton of spots.

That said, your lover is not off the hook—you want them to appreciate what you do. You don't want to feel like someone is taking advantage of you. More importantly, you want your partner to be a witness, watching all you do. They need to notice if the balance is getting upset and offer help in that moment when you truly need it. If you are overdoing it, your partner should say so. You want to feel like they're awake, aware, and connected to you.

A Sympathetic Ear

Even though they can completely run the show, Earth doesn't want to be in charge of everything in a romantic partnership. They want you to want to be involved. They want lots of talking through things, discussions, planning together. It might just be, "what's for dinner?", but they enjoy sharing this process. If you're a quiet person who likes to think a lot, this might be a lot more talking than you're used to, so you better start talking! The good news is if you do talk, Earth will listen.

One of Earth's greatest gifts is their ability to listen and validate. They can really understand their lover's problems, taking in a lover's story like food, chewing on it, digesting it, and transforming it and repeating it back to their partner in their own words. It's encouraging and uplifting, and it makes a person feel totally validated.

Everyone loves to be understood. Not only can you affirm a person, but if you're Earth, you can help solve their problems too. You have an amazing capacity for problem solving. This isn't a gut instinct kind of thing, the way Woods solve problems by jumping in and trying something. On the contrary, Earth is slow and patient.

As Earth, you approach challenges in life by first identifying the problem. Then you analyze the problem and all the possible solutions. This could take a very long time, but you are patient. You know from experience that taking your time means you're more likely to find the right answer to a problem the first time. Finally, you choose a solution based on your extensive analysis of the various options and potential outcomes. Whew! That's a lot of work. You approach problem solving as a process, and you know processes take time and patience. You're always up for the challenge, especially if you feel like you'll be appreciated.

This process-oriented approach is great for community building. Earth loves to be part of an intentional community that values treating each person with caring and dignity. Remember we mentioned President Obama was Earth? This is his style of leadership.

One Earth built an entire career out of interviewing people at various companies and schools, gathering tons of information, compiling all the gathered information, sifting and sorting it, and delivering uniform messages to the leaders of those institutions. It's the perfect Earth job. She gets to talk to people all day (the social component), and she has the patience to analyze and digest all that information, then transform it into something useful for people who don't have the patience to do that work. Her intelligence and skills are validated because she gets paid to do what she loves to do. And she loves being part of a team that contributes to the greater good.

Earth likes a democratic approach and makes sure everyone is included in decisions, especially their partner. They find out what people like and evaluate solutions that would meet everyone's need. At gatherings, they love to get a group to sit in a semi-circle so that all can be seen and heard. Earth holds the center to create a sacred space for the group, making it feel equal for everyone. They ensure that people sitting on the periphery (likely Metal) are invited into the fold. They take turns talking. They listen until the chosen speaker is finished with their thoughts, allow a pause, and then reply with their insights.

Agree to Disagree

If you're in a relationship with Earth, you might be surprised how easy it is for Earth to disagree with you. It's totally fine for two Earths to have differences of opinion. You can respect others' opinions without making them wrong and you right. And you can overcome differences and work out agreements through compromises. This is an Earth skill. They are the committee members who work hard and tirelessly to find agreement and harmony in their community.

In fact, one of their favorite activities is a big dinner party with lots of interesting, intellectual people. They love to be a part of a thought-provoking, dynamic, and exciting conversation in which each person's opinions and differences are welcomed. This is Earth's idea of a good time. It lights them up in a way they might not get in their day-to-day routine, and they come away thinking about the discussion for some time afterward.

Lifelong Learners

Earths love to learn and learn. They are the masters of the workshops, classrooms, and demonstrations. Why do they love to learn? Because they love to then share their knowledge. They are simply a catalyst in a process of transformation.

Earths are wonderful teachers both in the classroom and in life in general. They collect ideas and pieces of information. They hold these thoughts, put them in the EZ-Bake Oven of life, change the temperature, bake it, transform it, and give it to the right student who comes along. The concoction may have started out with a lot of different ingredients (knowledge bits) and ended up with that special cupcake of wisdom that made the recipient feel so loved and cared for.

However, a relationship with a teacher isn't always easy for the "student." Teacher-types want to teach you everything. If you're a grown adult, maybe you don't want any lessons today in laundry efficiency, grocery-shopping strategies, or proper leaf-raking techniques. If you say as much, now they're all hurt, with their tail between their legs. "I was just trying to *help* you," they'll say in a huff, and then go clean the gutters—most efficiently, of course.

Hurry Up and Ask Me

Although Earth gives humbly and selflessly, they sometimes recognize that they have to wait to be asked for help, especially in a relationship. Otherwise, they risk insulting the intelligence of the person they're trying to help. So they'll stand by and watch another person flounder when they're not asking for help. Often they feel as if their arms are full of all these gifts with no one to give them to. They can't just give gifts that don't match what a person needs—their gifts could be rejected. So Earth can feel unwanted or unneeded with so much to give and no one to receive it.

If you have an Earth partner, you might see yourself as the lucky recipient of all Earth's gifts. You might need to find a way to receive their teachings and understand without feeling like they're talking down to you. It's just a communication style. You can really benefit from all they know if you accept their gift without feeling slighted.

Try this as an experiment. Ask an Earth lover or friend for help with something that's frustrating you. Watch your friend's face light up like a twinkling star. Earth is so delighted when asked for help. They're ready to dive into the issue and evaluate the different solutions. They will then tell you about a specific product, technique, or class you need to take, and how it's perfect for your problem. While telling you the details, they will be animated, pleased, and energized by the act of giving you a solution.

Earths live and thrive for moments where they can help. They do all the legwork for people and are just looking for the people who are the right recipients for their brilliance and hard work.

Worry-Thwarted

Sometimes Earth gets shut down to all the goodness coming their way. This usually happens when they are worried. *Worry* shuts them down to all the abundance surrounding them. Worry is the bane of the Earth existence. It shuts down all that's coming in. It's like a tree that shuts out the sun and rain. They can be stuck on a problem for years, especially about a loved one, spending enormous amounts of time trying to figure out what to do. Being stuck for so long sucks the life out of everything else they want or try to do.

If you're in a relationship with an Earth, you can help them during these times of worry. You need to learn how to be a sounding board for them. Don't try to solve their problems for them. Earths are much better at solving problems than you could ever be. They've already thought of everything you're going to suggest anyway! They already know what the challenges are, but what they need is someone to talk to who can really listen. They need to talk out loud. This helps them discover the options that lead to the solution that has eluded them. Remember we mentioned they're the hard workers? They'll do the hard work. They just get derailed once in a while and need some support. It's time to give to the givers to get your Earth partner back on track.

Nicest Bitch Ever

Earths often say, "I don't understand it . . . I'm so nice to everyone out in the world, but I'm such a bitch at home." They feel ashamed of being like this because outside they are the nicest people they know! It's baffling. How can they be like that?

Surprisingly, Earth will often admit that they can be quite rude and even mean to anyone living with them. The trouble starts when they have to *ask* you to do your fair share of the work. You're supposed to be paying attention! You're supposed to see that work needs to be done and do it.

If they have to ask you to do something obvious or a chore you do regularly, that means the balance has been upset, and you were asleep and not noticing. Not noticing is a big no-no. You're supposed to be "partners"—that means *equal*. Hello! A partner is not a child. Even children don't get to behave like that. They are expected to do their chores. So where do you get off being so lazy?

Often when one person in a couple is Earth, the couple does really well until a child arrives. Children change the dynamic. Earth often expects to share the responsibilities of child rearing and wants the partner to be aware of what needs to be done. But when they start feeling that they're doing all the child rearing and housekeeping alone, they can get tired and overwhelmed. Then the resentment sets in. They even find they're taking out their frustrations on the children, which makes them doubly upset with their partner. The children need their nice parent back, not this mean one who has taken over. Then the finger pointing and blaming starts.

Earth partners don't want to be the ones always pointing out when things have gone awry. That makes them feel as if they're the only ones who care about the problems, and they start to look like a complainer. They aren't complainers. They are *fixers*. If their partner isn't helping to fix the problems with them, then they end up harping and barely recognizing themselves. No nooky-nooky is going to happen until the couple sorts their problem out.

Are You in Love with Earth?

No matter what your Element is, if you are partnered with Earth, here's a question to be asking your partner frequently: "You look really busy. Can I help?" The point is not what you do or how well you do it. The point is that you're noticing them and how much they're doing. You're noticing that they'd really like someone to just ask if they can do something for them even if they do it much better than you. You ask because you are sensitive to them, and you're watching them. It's saying, "I understand."

So how do you know if your partner is Earth? Earth is genuinely friendly, thoughtful, and caring. You can observe how your lover interacts with the world, through the eyes, the walk, and the sound of the voice. The way someone moves tells you about their Elemental Energy type.

The Walk: Shake It, Don't Break It

First, how does your lover walk? Earth walks with a gentle side-to-side rhythm, hips moving back and forth. The walk can be slow or fast, but most importantly, the feet must connect solidly to the ground. This is not a stomp, but a firm planting of the feet. They love walking barefoot to feel the connection with the ground beneath them.

You'll often notice their energy is centered in their belly, which may stick out even in the thinnest of Earths. It's like they have a Buddha belly, and they often rest their hands unconsciously on their bellies. There is circular nature to their walk. Their arms may sway, and their clothing may be loose and move with the air. They keep a rhythm or regular cadence when walking.

The Talk: Sweet Lullaby

Earth's voice is a storytelling voice that wants to convey the importance of particular thoughts and ideas with great seriousness. However, it can tend to lull people into sleep rather than excite them, due to its rhythmic quality.

Earth's words are sung in circular movement. Each word could make a drawn out circle. For example, when someone says, "anyway" so that it sounds like "an-y-waaay." The "way" syllable is extended for a few milliseconds longer. Or Earth can make a whole phrase or sentence circular. The bottom of the circle starts at the beginning of the phrase, it moves up in the middle, and comes back down at the end. The words flow gradually like a soothing lullaby, without harsh transitions, unlike the way the Fire's voice goes quickly and unpredictably up and down.

Each sentence has a rhythmical cadence, a pace that must be kept. Earth's sentences are long and elaborate. The voice extends out to you, and then draws you back into the speaker, as if you're being verbally hugged.

The Look: Bambi Eyes

Earth eyes are soft and round like a doe's. Because their gift is the ability to listen to people, they tend to open their eyes wide in a way that fully takes in the person they are looking at. Their soft eyes say, "Go ahead, I'm listening."

Or they may cock their head to the side, presenting an ear to the speaker to show they are really listening. If what you're telling them is troublesome, they may knit their eyebrows together to convey a sense of concern or worry.

What Does Earth Want— Listening to Your Soul

Every Element is best at what it wants most, and Earth is the best listener. In fact, Earth listens at such a deep level that most of us have no idea what they hear. At this level of presence, they are listening intently, as if to vibrations. They have to have a stillness inside to hear at this level. They are penetrating to the still point at the center of everything so they can hear what you are truly saying, what's behind your words. They hear your soul speaking.

So what do they want most? All they want is for someone to just listen to what they have to say. What they want is a person to listen so deeply that the person takes in what they're saying, processes it, and then restates it in their own words. This restatement is validation for how they are feeling. It's as if they come to know themselves more deeply through this connection that is created by the feeling of, "You *get* me." Being "gotten" or validated means a person was able to extrapolate what the Earth is saying to actually come to a deeper conclusion than Earth even originally stated. It is the ultimate in validation and understanding.

Because the world often isn't listening to them, Earths are sometimes accused of being needy. They absolutely hate to be characterized this way, and as a result, often try to appear completely self-sufficient, never asking for help.

The Evolution of Earth

So many times Earths fall into the trap of wanting and relying on romantic lovers to give them what they need—validation, appreciation, and understanding. Alas, your loved ones often fall short. In the evolution of Earth, you come to realize that the only person who can really satisfy your need for validation is yourself. Instead of having expectations for others, you come to believe that you yourself or some divine power will fulfill your needs. It's a surrendering, a trust. It can take Earth a lifetime to figure this out.

Once you learn to listen and validate yourself, giving and receiving can stay in balance. You no longer look for people who can satisfy your needs. People no longer disappoint you. And you can give of yourself freely without expecting any gifts in return and without resentment. This is a tall order because it is easy to resent all the other Elements who are takers out there. But once you feel fulfilled in yourself and learn how to completely take in all the goodness of the universe in a constant stream, then you no longer need to withhold anything of yourself.

Give to the world, Earth, and receive from the universe. You deserve it!

Six

Metal—
Crowd Surfing
Through Life

....

"Have you ever watched a leaf leave a tree?
It falls upwards at first, and then it drifts toward
the ground, just as I find myself drifting towards you.
Beth Kephart, from Undercover

....

What do James Dean, Marilyn Monroe, Angelina Jolie, and
Johnny Depp all have in common? A mysterious magnetism that intoxicates us into wanting them ... plus the fact

that they are Metal. For some reason, this is incredibly sexy and desirable because over and over, the most legendary people in our pop culture seem to be Metal.

Is it the clothes? Is it the style? Is it the fact that they don't seem to care about what people think of them? No, it's more than that. It's the way their arms just hang off their body, the way they look as though they're walking on clouds like kings or queens, their unfocused eyes, even a nonchalant stroke of the hand to brush the hair from their eyes. They mesmerize the rest of us. Their eyes seem to have x-ray vision seeing right through you, unnerving you. They see through your masks and pretentious ways, right to the core.

Metals are not particularly outgoing or bold, but they have a rebellious quality that makes them stand out. They hang back and let the world come to them. Metal makes us curious; they make us want to find out more. They hang out, often reclining in a chair, watching the unfolding of life in front of them. At a party, they don't greet people at the door. They wait for folks to come to them. They put the cool in "cool factor" because they don't have to try to be cool—they just *are*.

If you're Metal, the rest of the world is enamored with your mysteriousness. It's like you have a direct connection with some kind of divine ethereal realm the rest of us can't access. So we want to be near you in the hope that something in you might rub off on us. We want to figure you out, to find out what's inside all the mystery.

Entering the Sacred
Temple of Life, Respectfully

If you're Metal and you walk into a temple or cathedral, do you enter laughing boisterously with friends? No, you come in quietly, reverently, unassuming, head bowed slightly. In fact, that's true for almost everything you do—as if the whole entire world were your temple. You walk through life watching respectfully, paying attention to what's happening around you, aware of even the air you breathe. You're connected to something that isn't visible, yet cosmic. Nature is an exquisite, sublime painting—a meditation on beauty. You look for value; you connect with what's most sacred, beautiful, and worthy of appreciation.

Now imagine you're walking into a rock concert, which is your temple for the night. Inside you are pumped and fired up, but outside everyone else just sees you as total coolness. You're decked out in the latest cutting-edge fashion, which could easily be leather and studs for this night. You look like you really don't care about life the way others do. This is a cavalier, I-don't-give-a-shit-because-I-have-better-things-to-think-about attitude. It's like you just float through life on a magic carpet, riding gusts of wind that take you hither and thither. In a way, you're crowd surfing, jumping off the stage at the concert. You completely let go into free fall, and for a fleeting moment you trust that by some miracle, someone will be there to stop you from falling. And as the crowd catches you, holds you, moves and passes you around, you are limp and trusting. You are just so cool.

Now imagine you're making love. Your bed becomes your sacred temple. When you make a connection, you can look into your lover's eyes with unwavering love, and your eyes can well up with tears of appreciation. You recognize that your deep and sacred connection with this person is fleeting, but you are in the moment right there and now. You love the things you know won't last even more *because* they are impermanent. At the heart of it, you know this lover is only a passenger on your magic carpet who might, at any moment, disembark. And once again, you completely let go into free fall, into the arms of your lover, easy and connected. Smooth operator.

Death Becomes You

As Metal, you innately know that everything comes to an end. This is the energy of autumn when the plants return to the earth so that they can sprout again in the spring. You respect this cycle. Metal is more in tune with this transition to death that awaits every living thing than any of the other Elemental Energy types. And for this reason, if you are Metal, you live life to the fullest. You have to connect with something greater than all of us in every moment to be truly living.

This means you have an ability to cut through bullshit. You see beyond the phoniness and inauthenticity people present to the world. You're not afraid of the down-and-dirty and the nitty-gritty of things. You are 100 percent real while the rest of the world can seem to you to be playing a silly game. You sit back and watch, making connections with the few people who let down their guard and sit by your side, enjoying this moment in time, before once again things change, and you move on.

Cool Zen, Hollywood Style

Our culture is fascinated with cool celebrities. Marilyn Monroe and James Dean almost dared us to want to get to know them more. They both really wanted to become respected actors and worked hard at their acting craft, all the while seemingly being tormented by the outside world. Everyone wanted a piece of their elusive brand of coolness, and to this day, they are still desired and thought of as sexy. Today, we have the sultry and quiet sexiness of Johnny Depp and Angelina Jolie. Both are box office sensations who are always searching for deeper characters to portray in film. These are not ordinary people. They are quiet, honoring, and always watching the world we all live in.

Meryl Streep, one of the most celebrated actors of our time, is also Metal. She takes on so many different characters in her films, but her unnerving deep eyes reveal her Elemental Energy type. What makes her such an amazing actor is that she brings her respect for her characters to the screen. She makes them larger than life. For example, she devotes herself to becoming Julia Child in *Julie & Julia*, in a way that honors Child more than any award or accolade has ever done. We have seen her transform into so many great women on the big screen, but rarely see her as herself on TV or in interviews. Coincidently, starring with Meryl Streep in *Julie & Julia* was Jane Lynch, who also happens to be Metal.

The list of Metal actors through the years goes on and on: Greta Garbo, Humphrey Bogart, and many more.

Connecting to the Cosmic Connection

What is connection, really? How do you connect with something that is cosmic in nature?

The Metal way of connection is not like the heart-to-heart connection we see with Fire. Fires open their hearts to you to make a connection. The Metal way of connection is to talk quietly, one on one. It's much more like a cosmic or divine connection with something greater than us.

Hanging out with people facilitates the connection. Metal can actually get very close and use touch to help find the cosmic connection, bringing about a feeling of awe and deep appreciation. It comes from the sense of being in the presence of some person, place, or thing of greater value.

How does anyone know the true value of something? One way to appreciate something fully is by imagining or experiencing the idea of not having it. What would life be like without that person, place, or thing? The amount of longing you experience can strengthen connection to it when it is again present.

Metals treat people deemed worthy with the utmost respect. The way to display this respect is not with an exuberance and high-five Wood cheerleading. That kind of reaction can send a Metal person heading for the hills. For Metal, words are not needed. A silent head nod, a solemn expression, hands in prayer position, a bowing gesture, a connection through the eyes is enough. The eyes say, "I appreciate you. I respect you. I value you." What they want most in life is for folks to value them through this type of respectfulness.

The Metal Element is associated with the lungs and breathing. When Metal takes a breath, their soul appears to reach up to heaven and make a connection, as if they are inhaling inspiration from the greater cosmos. In every breath, they connect. They have this innate sense of oneness with all, and they make the people they love feel so cherished and special. They treat them with the reverence with which they would treat themselves.

Breathing In to Say Goodbye

After every breath in we must exhale. Breathing out symbolizes the loss of connection that happens all day, every day with everything. Life is ever changing. Nothing can be sustained forever. After taking in the breath, energy moves downward through the body and dissipates as all the breath is again released.

Without that perspective of loss, people might take things for granted. Metal's distinctive virtue and plight is to be acutely aware of the impermanence of life. All things change and become something else. Nothing is stagnant in the universe. In the connection, Metal embraces the now in the awareness that it is ephemeral and will surely give way to something else in the future.

It's like the sublime moment when the orange brilliance of a sunset is at its lowest in the sky. The encroaching darkness surrounds the orange at this glorious moment just before swallowing up its beauty, disappearing in a poof. This is how Metal sees life—fleeting, ephemeral. The settling into darkness is easy and comfortable. It's not sad. It's what is supposed to be. And letting go of the sun is something they do every day.

Soft on the Outside, Strong on the Inside

The Metal exterior is like soft puffy clouds, not the armor you'd expect. In fact they don't feel protected from the onslaught of the world. They feel sensitive to other people's energy and noises in general. They often avoid crowds because of their sensitive soft outside. Greta Garbo was notorious for hiding under her hat and coat in New York City, even running from her fans for decades.

Metals don't usually assert themselves in the world. They are the opposite of Wood's assertiveness. Some Metals have Wood second and are more assertive than other Metals, but even then they hold back more often than not.

Don't mistake the soft exterior for weakness, however. Far from it, on the inside they are as strong as steel, especially when push comes to shove. They tend to wait patiently for things. If they are annoyed or upset, they will try not to do or say anything unless their discontent becomes unbearable. Due to the delay, their frustration can mount until it can't be held in any longer. Then all that strength inside them can come out with explosive force, often shocking those around them. When they are pushed into a confrontation, they will easily defeat anyone who is macho and full of bravado, like Wood, for example. Metal chops Wood, so to speak. Because it takes a lot of effort for that strength inside to come out, it can be surprising and effective.

Judge the Crime, Not the Criminal

In Chinese history, Metal played the role of the judge. Being a judge doesn't mean you're judgmental. On the contrary, Metal simply looks at the facts and judges whether the law has been broken. The stories behind why the person needed to break the law are irrelevant. The question is simple: Was the law broken? It's a binary question, not a multiple choice. The laws are black and white. True or false. There is no debate. Judges have little or no emotional attachment to the outcome, which suits Metal just fine.

Metals follow the laws of the land with due respect for them, so they won't fudge or abuse them. Metals are not the type to create a parking space where one doesn't exist. Instead, they'll happily walk the extra distance from the back of the parking lot. In fact, they wish they could be the ones writing parking tickets to all disrespectful people who do park illegally.

Because they respect the rules, they have the ability to work in large organizations where there are lots of procedures and processes to follow. They can be bureaucrats and push paper all day. Some may enjoy the routine, but others would prefer not to have to belong to something. They tend to want to fly solo whenever possible. They'd rather sit outside the circle and watch everyone interact. By and large, they're not joiners. They don't like being labeled, and they like to be different.

Although they are deeply spiritual and reverent, they can also have an irreverent quality. They have a dry sense of humor, slightly caustic and sarcastic. Absurdities are a delight. Playing with disappointment in humor can be very funny. Think of the comedy of Bill Murray and Jim Gaffigan. With a twisted viewpoint, they are always disappointed with life. They skillfully point out people's foibles and the life's irony.

Metal has a quiet sense of rebelliousness. They feel different from everyone else and have a sense of wanting to somehow exhibit that difference to others. The punk rock movement of the late 1970s and 1980s is a perfect Metal analogy. How best than through music and fashion? The black leather and body piercings created a tough mystique on the outside.

It was as if they were worried that their cloudy, misty exterior would be mistaken for weakness. So they adopted a fashion statement that said, "We may not look tough, but we are tough on the inside. So don't mess with us."

There is a delicate balance between these two extremes of obeying the rules and being rebellious. Metal actually hates to be all nicey-nice but find themselves being nice all the time because they don't want to make people uncomfortable. They get in trouble when they are annoyed but feel the *need* to be nice. Their annoyance can build until they go from very nice to not nice at all.

The Lose-Lose

Playing by the rules doesn't mean you're playing to win. Metal is not about winning the game, but about reaching your personal best—even when your personal best is the best score on the board, Metal sees it as the place where you lost for the day. For example, if you are a long distance runner and beat your personal best, you haven't really won; you've only discovered a new place for improvement. You never truly win.

For this reason, Metal may frame their language much more often around losing than winning. If their team wins a game, they might point out what didn't work and where the disappointment occurred. Even if they are very happy with the win, they still focus on where there is room for improvement.

Love and Metal

A dog may be a man's best friend, but Metal is a close second as a loyal BFF in the romance department. They are devout in their love for you. They love with a connection that is very steadfast and true, and they will honor and protect you. They will go the distance for you.

Sure, youth may override the desire to be in a long-term relationship, and they may have many lovers. Remember, they are the epitome of cool. Everyone wants to be with them. But if that one person comes along that kisses them cosmically, they can be hopelessly romantic.

Although many are often chasing them, occasionally Metal may pursue another person. But more often they wait for the rest of the world to come to them. Unfortunately, this might mean they don't have many Metal friends. When two Metals want to be friends, one of them must be forced to make the effort ... pick up the phone, send that email, walk across the room. The best friendships between two Metal people happen when they're in some kind of program or living situation where they have chance encounters. Then they gravitate toward each other naturally because they feel so comfortable not having to talk, just being together and speaking about offhand unusual things, almost cryptically (to any outsiders).

So if you want to develop a new romantic relationship with Metal, you might want to pick up the phone and call them. Otherwise, you might be waiting a long time to hear from them. Hopefully life will make it easy for you and give you reasons to see each other often. But other than that, you may find you have to pursue the relationship.

Be careful and make sure your desired lover really is into you if you're doing all the pursuing. Metal can sometimes hang with people, even lovers, and not really be in love. You pursued them, and they let you. But it doesn't mean they're in love with you. If they are feeling very romantic and excited, they are into you. If they look half-bored all the time, well, then they probably are bored.

If you sit with Metal, you can be very close to that person, right up against them. They are comfortable with close contact. Your touch and closeness might fill them with a sense of connection, making tears well up in their eyes. They are filled with an appreciation for your presence in that fleeting moment.

Hot Metal to the Touch

For Metal, the world is an experience waiting to happen. It's full of sights, smells, tastes, and sensations of touch. When having an experience of the senses, Metal feels present and connected.

So there's nothing that compares to the sense of connection Metal feels when having sex. Sex with Metal is an experience of all the senses at once!

Having an experience of connection and presence with a lover means you don't want to rush anything. Fast and furious doesn't honor the precious moment of being in connection. Your bed becomes your church. You move slowly with consideration at all times of the other person. You ease into the sensations and really feel what is happening. The connection may or may not involve the eyes (like Fire uses the eyes). Your hands become your eyes. You feel the other person's presence through touch. In fact, closing your eyes may enhance the tactile sensations.

The Knight Errant of Love

Metal in romance is like the Knight Errant of Love. Think Camelot, Lancelot, and medieval chivalry. These knights rode out into the countryside looking for good deeds to do in the name of their Lady. Now that's romantic! The knight works alone and needs no one. This is the life of Metal, to be in service when necessary but be solitary much of the time. Nowadays, the knight errant can be just as romantic, male or female. Their exploits may not be as dramatic as fighting dragons, but they still like to slay you in the bedroom!

Metal is very inquisitive in lovemaking. They seek out new things to experience all the time. But they don't just try it once and move on. Oh no! Again and again and again, they want to experience this newfound pleasure. It may be fun for the next five times too. And if they're really enjoying themselves, they may try it from many angles and in many ways, exploring something thoroughly and experiencing all its nuances. Metal is all about nuances and new sensations.

There is a difference between experiencing the senses and being sensual. Sensuality (which is the Earth Element) is about really being in touch with a lover's needs and having an innate grasp of what that is. Metal is truly about the sublime experience of touch, sound, taste, sight, and smell.

The Leaf Leaves the Tree ... Forever

When something or someone is lost, for whatever reason, Metal's challenge is to let it go. Metals are constantly faced with the letting go, detaching, moving on to wherever the next breeze takes them.

Think back on all that you've loved. Is it really gone? Can you conjure it up again and feel the same feelings you did when you had it? If so, you know that time and space cannot separate you once you've made a connection. This is a state of nostalgia. It's a pleasurable feeling to remember loved ones of the past. It's the feeling of being full of appreciation for something that was precious. A connection might also be with a friend, relative, lover, or an object, such as a something with sentimental meaning.

Metal can be the most steadfast friend. No distance or time can take away their connection. You may not have spoken for years and live three thousand miles away from your Metal friend, but they continue to be connected to you. Metal has the ability to remember what connected them in the first place.

The only time Metals break that connection is if you violate their trust. Once that happens, it's very hard for them to connect again. And really, Metals lose their self-respect if they continue to be your friend after you've violated their trust.

The nightmare situation for Metal is when they lose the connection with something or someone they are attached to and can't let go of. They become focused what they are leaving behind. Then they can no longer appreciate something new because they're crying about a past relationship.

This condition can be very serious, sometimes life threatening. Everyone grieves when a loved one dies, but Metals may lose their perspective on life when something incredibly valuable is lost. This is not nostalgia, which can feel good in a soft, subtle way. It can be a very intense bereavement that is not a healthy way to experience grief. When stuck in this pattern of refusing to let go and detach, Metals can be susceptible to an unhealthy intensity.

It is not unique to them; everyone grieves. But Metal, when stuck in this pattern of refusing to let go and detach, can be susceptible to an unhealthy intensity.

Metals have a choice. Either enjoy life's ride in a state of detachment or experience misery when the inevitable losses of life, big or small, pile up one on top of another.

When you view life as ephemeral and temporary, you can try to cling to everything you cherish, which means a life of sadness when everything leaves you in the end. Or you can rejoice in every connection and realize that you never truly lose anything once you've made the connection. The memory is yours. The nostalgia that fills you with a quiet joy is yours for all eternity.

Keepers of the Peace and Quiet

Metal is easily annoyed by boisterous, peace-disturbing activities. They often do not want to go to carnivals, festivals, or boring potlucks. Yet, strangely enough, ask them to go to a rock concert and they are *so* there. It's not like they want to be party-poopers since they do love to party. But they really need a lot more time alone at home than the other Elements. Sometimes in love relationships, they keep their complaints to themselves because they feel guilty about raining on someone else's parade. But then they feel very uncomfortable, and tension begins to build inside until something tips them over the edge and they have an outburst. Family members may feel like they're walking on eggshells around Metal. And this makes Metal feel even worse since they really are nice and care about other people's feelings.

It's important for anyone in a love relationship with Metal to be respectful and ask them questions often, keeping the communication lines open. It's really about being considerate and respectful of their sensitivity to noise and their need to have alone time. Metal needs to feel comfortable enough in the relationship to speak the truth before their annoyance festers and boils up.

Are You in Love with Metal?

Metal is laid back and chill. They make you want to slow down and smell the roses of life, appreciating what matters most. But how can you tell if your partner is Metal? You can observe how your lover interacts with the world, through the eyes, the walk, and the sound of the voice. The way someone moves tells you about their Elemental Energy type.

The Walk: Walking on Clouds

The easiest thing to notice is Metal's shoulders are pushed back and squared off. This gives their lungs maximum breathing capacity. They stand upright with their head held up high, so the top of their head is reaching to the sky. It's as if they are dangling on a string from the heavens above. Like a puppet, the arms usually dangle loosely at the sides as everything descends down from the top of their heads. Some may look like their nose is up in the air a slight bit (with an air of regalness). Their feet hardly touch the ground when they walk, making it look like those feet are walking on clouds, with a silent footfall.

The Talk: Eeyore on a Good Day

Listening to Metal might give you the impression that they are about to break down crying at any moment. However, they rarely cry. It's simply that you hear a little catch in their voice, a crackle that people who are about to cry often make.

Eeyore, Winnie the Pooh's friend, is Metal perpetually having a bad day. His cartoon voice is an over-stated example of Metal, but a great learning tool to hear the characteristics of descending vocals. And Eeyore's so cute!

Metal's voice goes up for an instant just after they take a breath. Then as they speak, the voice begins a long descent downward until it can hardly be heard. Then the person finally takes another breath, and voilà! The voice can be heard again.

The voice can be breathy, as if there's not enough air to speak. It can either be gentle and heavy or sometimes sounds like a bell ringing, with crystalline clarity.

They tend to often eliminate unimportant words in sentences, as if the pronouns, articles, and prepositions are just way too much effort to say. Try this out in your best Eeyore voice, *"This writing business. Pencils and whatnot. Overrated if you ask me. Silly stuff. Nothing in it."*—Eeyore

The Eyes: Defocusing on You

Metal eyes have x-ray vision. They look straight through you as if they are focused on some point beyond you in the not too far off distance. They are essentially defocused.

Even though Metal rarely cries, they often look like they have tears in their eyes when they make a cosmic connection with someone or something close by. A fleeting nostalgic thought fills them with reverence.

What Does Metal Want?

Metal believes that at the core of their beings they are like a priceless gem. They know they are valuable. On a good day, they don't care what anyone else thinks, which is why the world seemingly always wants more from them. But sometimes when they are off, they feel defeated and want to give up trying. They have a woe-is-me outlook on life, which can lead to a need to impress the world, proving their value.

What they want from their circle of friends, loved-ones, and colleagues is acknowledgment of their worth, the respect and honor they feel they've earned. Small gestures go a long way in acknowledging the honorable Metal as when everyone stands quietly when the judge walks into the courtroom in a silent sign of respect.

In romance, Metal most wants to fly on a magic carpet ride with a partner, side-by-side in mutual respect and quiet consideration. In tandem, you together experience the vibrations of the music, savor the amazing tastes, and feel the velvety touch of the skin along your journey. Metal is acutely aware that we have exited out of the cosmic mystery of the unknown to be born into this life and that we all exist on borrowed time. Hopefully, for Metal, it will be a wild, crazy, and very cool ride before entering back into death.

The Evolution of Metal

When Metals are searching for the approval of others, they are *not* free to be fully themselves. They cannot simply seek or demand respect. In order to be respected, they must first be respectful to others. Take teachers, for example. Why do students love a particular teacher more than others? Often it's the Metal teacher who treats students with consideration and respect. The students give their respect to the ones who respect them most.

The evolution of Metal is to be of service in every situation, even if the people you are serving don't appreciate your efforts. Without worrying about needing to be respected in turn, you hold the place of honor by doing what is honorable regardless of the rewards. In other words, feeling honorable comes from your sense of yourself, not how the world sees you. Honor comes from within.

As the valiant knight's sword cuts through negativity, bringing purity and inspiration to all ... so does Metal. Though these knights often walk alone, romantic love motivates them. And for this reason they easily win the love of others. They are the *hopeful* romantics of the Elemental world!

Thank you, Metal, for your service. This moment of silence is for you.

Seven

Water—Sexual Tsunami

....

"Trust yourself. Create the kind of self that
you will be happy to live with all your life.
Make the most of yourself by fanning the tiny,
inner sparks of possibility into flames of achievement."

Golda Meir

....

Are you ready? No, really, we mean *really* ready? Are you
ready for anything to happen at any moment? Water is ready
for life—its unpredictability, the way it's constantly changing, and the fact that you have no control over what's next,
really. Most people think they know what is going to happen
next in life, but only Water is truly ready for anything. They

have the energy and know-how to deal with it all. Water is the go-to Element for readiness.

Imagine you have a big, powerful engine embedded in your lower back. You're at a stoplight, revving your engine, vroom, vroom ... Right now, this very moment, all the excitement is in the anticipation of the light turning green. It's about being ready to move. The biggest thrill is in waiting and watching before the light turns, not the actual moment after you put the pedal to the metal. The thrill is being alive and ready for the moment, any moment, when the state of waiting changes to the state of movement.

Water is the energy of forward moving without stopping and retreating. It may come from a high place, such as the mountains, and descend down to the valleys below. Does it only take one path down? No. A superhighway? No. Water finds many ways down, multiple brooks and streams on its way to the ocean. It meanders, takes detours, splits off and then finds its way back to the bigger rivers.

Once water finds the lowest ground, it continues forward relentlessly without stopping—a meandering river always finds its way to the ocean. When a rushing river of Water comes your way like an unstoppable freight train, it's best to either jump on board or get out of the way!

The ocean symbolizes the true scope of the variety of movement in the Water Element. At the surface of the ocean is this incredible activity and movement. The waves are in constant and relentless motion. Underneath, the deeper you go, the more still things become. Stillness is at the bottom. But there's something else at the bottom. The more still things get, the more power is amassed. Tsunamis don't start on the surface. They start at the bottom of the ocean, at the exact moment they cannot remain still any longer.

If you're Water, it's likely that you alternate between times of intense activity and times of peace and recuperation? One day you might be like a still pond, amassing energy so that you can utilize it for intense movement when the time is right.

The Cool Before It's Cool

Do you know that anything can happen at any moment? Are you prepared for the unknown? Can you instantly mobilize for anything urgent, like jumping out of your chair in a split second to catch a precious falling object? Do you like to stand out and be different? Are you happy doing something really intense and then resting for days afterwards? Are you innately spontaneous, and do you love to do something silly?

If you want to go take a nap or go lie down after answering all these questions or you just want to answer them later when you have more energy, you're likely Water, or you have Water in your top three elements. (Okay, we're just kidding here a little.)

Water is about hesitating and waiting, then surging forward with power, skill, and know-how. They're constantly alternating between being stillness and sudden surges of movement. Don't mistake the quiet look for shyness! Water is shy-*looking* one minute, and courageous another moment. When Water has a romantic interest, they may not look as if they're going to ask for a date, until suddenly they pop the question with boldness that can be surprising.

Water knows that anything can happen at any moment. They're not normally afraid of something bad happening. They don't plan, like Earth does. What's the point of planning for something specific when at any moment everything could change? They're simply prepared for anything to happen. They often gravitate toward careers such as EMT technicians, emergency personnel, firefighters, and police officers. They all spend periods of time waiting and then periods of time in intense activity, after which they rest and recharge before starting again.

Dare to Be Different

Are you interested in doing a lot of things? Is your sense of fashion daring and eclectic? Let's call it the "Dare to Be Different" style. Sometimes it can look nerdy or geeky. Other times stylish and trendy. But one thing is for sure, if it's quirky, hipster, or a just-off-the-mark look—it is probably a Water under those clothes. Think stylish Water Justin Timberlake and all of his various looks that put a spark in men's fashion and a smile on women's faces.

Then there's the highlight (or lowlight) of the Watery fashion faux pas Björk made when she wore a swan dress to the Oscars (Google it to see the photos!). The garment has been called one of the most iconic Oscar dresses of all time. For good or bad, it was a Water fashion gamble. Björk, whose music is extreme Water, was unapologetic to the fashion critics. She wore the dress because she loved swans and dared to be different. Case closed.

Waters can end up being the coolest trendsetters, by just being daring enough to wear or do whatever they like. They've been called fashion forward, trendsetters or hipsters, wearing things before they are popular. (On a side note…For some bizarre reason, no one wants to be called a hipster…but the Metals and Waters have to own it. A hipster merges Metal sarcasm and nostalgia for the past with Water's love of irony and the absurd.)

While the fashion trendsetters can sometimes be Metal (think Johnny Depp's eclectic but very cool style), more times than not, the person is a bold and brave Water taking the leap. The difference between Metal fashion and Water fashion is that whatever Metal is wearing is just cool. They make something new look like it's already "in," even if it isn't yet. Often Water wears something that looks maybe too offbeat and even awkward, but if they pull it off, you'll want to try it out. They have the courage to be first, so they really stand out.

Raining Comedy

A huge percentage of famous comedians are Water. Jack Black, Jim Carrey, Robin Williams, Whoopi Goldberg, Adam Sandler, Wanda Sykes, Russell Brand, Kevin Hart…the list goes on and on. Their humor is ironic, quirky, and off-the-wall funny. Water loves to make people laugh.

Since childhood, Water has been told to sit still and be quiet. But inside they want to burst out and let loose. So it makes sense that they take to the stage where they can be rewarded and appreciated for silly slapstick comedy and being spastic. What a great way for Water to unleash its powers. No one ever tells them to tone it down on stage.

Even the biggest Water celebrities appear to have a great sense of humor—Justin Timberlake, Zooey Deschanel, Jay-Z, Channing Tatum, Demi Moore, and Quentin Tarantino (yes, even in his most violent scenes, he finds a place to insert his quirky sense of humor). Water people also show up in other walks of life. Famous artist Tom Friedman (Water) pushes the boundaries of the seriousness of the art world with his ironic and sometimes comical sculptures.

Foot Tappers and Wigglers

What you see on the outside with Water is not what's happening on the inside. When they move with intensity through exercise or during an emergency, Water feels a sense of stillness and calm on the inside. Conversely, if they're required to be completely still on the outside, the energy builds up, swirling around inside them. For this reason, they often can't sit still in social settings, bouncing their legs or tapping their pens in social settings. The more restrained their movement the more antsy they can get. When you put a kink in a garden hose to stop the water flow, the water can end up busting a hole somewhere else. You just can't stop Water. Eventually it will find a way to flow.

Hurry Up and Slow Down

Waters come in two modes. The first type of Water never stops moving, like the river rapids. They are in near constant motion. If you ask them to do something, they put everything down the moment you ask and frantically do it right then, even if you don't need it done for a few days. One woman complained she has to remember *not* to ask her husband to do something until just before she really needs it done. Otherwise he does things too soon. (And in rare cases, this type of Water can be obsessively tidy.) And you're probably thinking…"And this is something to complain about? I wish my partner would jump when I say 'jump!'" But for the partners of fast-moving Waters, their quickness can be exasperating. To make the relationship work, the partner will have to figure out how to adapt to their rapid response times.

The second type of Water is very chill. They take a long time to be motivated to do something different than what they're doing in the moment. You might have to ask them ten times to do something for you, or it may take four years to clean the garage, the shed, or their car. They're like the trickling spring bubbling up but not going anywhere too fast. This can be exasperating, and partners end up feeling that they have to nag or look the other way.

And even when Water gets to it, it can take them forever to do the task. So they put it off until it has to be done or until they feel like doing it. Normally, if someone cleans a room, it might take an hour at most, right? If your partner is

Water, it may take four hours (unless they're the super speedy type, which means they're already done with their chore and on to the next one or they're taking a nap!). This is because they do it slowly and with a lot of intense focus. They do it very thoroughly and until the job's done right, which is why they think they're the best cleaners. They don't just vacuum—they vacuum every nook and cranny possible. Just the vacuuming alone could take an hour!

Even though they might think they're clean, their cars may tell a different story. Water's tendency is to spill out all over the place. They need a lot of things close by and handy so they can respond to anything the universe throws at them. Now we know why trunks were really invented—for Waters to put their "valuables" in. WD-40? Got it. Philips head screw driver? Got it. Emergency flare? Got it. Old blanket? Got it. Old collectible poetry books? Got it. A month's worth of Starbucks cups? Got it. Four umbrellas of various sizes? Got it. Six golf balls? Got it. (If you do complain about their "collection," they'll say, "This thing might save your butt someday!") They aren't dirty; they just don't see that things are out of their place. Water is the element of disorganization or lack of boundaries. It is chaos on wheels.

Raging River of Love

Waters are zoned into whatever they're doing in life. If they're in love, they're totally into it. Head over heels, no holds barred. They live life in the now moment and completely give themselves over to it. Especially if you like attention, being the recipient of their romantic focus can be really great. But even when you're in love, when Water is focused in tently on something *else*, a break from the intensity can be very welcome. Love may take a back seat for a while. For some, that much intensity on a lover can actually be very tiring. Balance between intensity and inactivity is the key to healthy love affairs with Water.

Are you attracted to Water? Maybe you feel your life is a little boring. People are very attracted to Water's spontaneity, unpredictability, and sense of humor. It's exciting to be with people who can be so changeable. Water might be running off to exotic places to climb up, jump off, or rappel down something. You know the type. The advertising campaigns for Mountain Dew, Red Bull, and ESPN X-Games, just to name a few, are all aimed at adventure seekers, extreme athletes, and video gamers, aka Water.

And they love to have company in whatever they're doing. They might be really into something, let's say rock climbing. Maybe you like rock climbing too. They'll love to have you share their adventures with them. They connect with people more through doing stuff and less through talking.

Kinesthetic Sense

A kinesthetic sense can be described as a keen, almost unconscious ability to know from memory how to do something well. Gymnasts, dancers, and many athletes all have this ability. It's like knowing unequivocally that you hit the golf ball perfectly before it even hits the green. It's feeling that sweet spot, like some kind of knowing where you literally feel what's going to happen. Tiger Woods is the ultimate example of Water's kinesthetic sense every time he steps on the golf course. In the love department, however, Tiger's kinesthetic sense may have caused him a bit of trouble!

On the dance floor, Water uses their kinesthetic sense to get to know people deeply through movement and touch. What better way to get to know a romantic interest than on the dance floor? Or making love? Both dancing and sex allow Waters to touch while moving and feeling the other person against their bodies. In this way they can feel to the depths of a partner's soul without having to "think." They sense a connection that is strong but fluid. Dancing is like making love standing up. There's a reason why the latest dance shows on TV are so popular. You can sit on the couch (resting and rejuvenating) while watching other people dance provocatively. A sexy socially acceptable dose of voyeurism that you can tune in to weekly on your favorite station, perhaps?

High-Intensity Couch Potatoes

These days, you don't even have to leave home to have an adventure. If you're living with a Water partner, don't be surprised to find them on the couch for numerous hours some days. But the question is why? With video games Waters get to sit down and be still while driving race cars, shooting the enemy, or playing on the same team as major league athletes. Water is the perfect TV audience. Heck, video games are made for Water; they get to replenish their energy sitting while participating in intense mental adrenaline spikes playing for hours.

The adrenal glands in Chinese Medicine are directly related to Water. They give Water their power. With an adrenaline rush in an emergency, people can have enough superhuman strength to miraculously lift a car off of someone at a crash site. Water can be especially powerful because they constantly protect their adrenaline (by resting after periods of intense action). You might hear a nearly exhausted Water say, "I just need to lie down," or "I'm saving up my energy reserves." And nothing taps your adrenaline like hot, fun sex!

Predicting Unpredictability

Sex with Water is unpredictable, spontaneous, and carefree. One Water woman said she'd much rather have sex in an elevator than in bed. But she admits that even though she thinks about doing it in an elevator, in reality she probably wouldn't feel safe enough to do it.

Water loves to take risks that feel safe, and every Water has a different idea of safety. So one Water might think sex in a public place is a total thrill because they might get caught. Another might be mortified to get caught. Stuck in their fear, they don't allow themselves the freedom to actually do it.

No matter what their level of safety is, they like to push their own envelope. One woman forced herself to go skydiving even though she really hated it once she did. She just really wanted to push herself, and she knew she'd be safe.

She needed drama and intensity to balance her stagnant life. Hmmm, now we're thinking maybe she should have tried sex while skydiving—it might have been even more fun!

Unpredictability means no predictable rhythm, right? Don't try to predict a Water person. Sex once or twice a week is too predictable. Water follows lots of different rhythms in their life. Expect this randomness to flow into the bedroom too. One woman says her Water husband will make mad passionate love to her ten days in a row, and then weeks might pass before they have sex again. Water focuses on doing one thing for an extended time… it might be work, or a hobby, or lovemaking. But they do it to the max. Until their focus shifts to something else.

Water interests are so varied that it's impossible to know what they will like sexually. But one thing's for sure, their sex life won't be boring. If it is, that's out of fear that they would upset their partner. If they don't feel safe to be themselves in the relationship, then they might contain themselves and not be spastic or silly. They'll find small ways to create laughter and exciting moments outside the bedroom.

When the Dam Breaks

Remember, Water is about power, and power is about constant motion. They often pursue their romantic interests with energy and enthusiasm. Many people find this quality very hot, sexy, and passionate. Moving quickly, Water's power floods their lovers with energy. But Water also likes their lovers to alternate in sharing the power. They're interested in someone who can match their intensity in bed. These power dynamics can put even more gusto into their sex.

Water is incredibly playful and silly, catching their partner off-guard, at inopportune moments. "Really, here? On the kitchen counter?" "Yes, yes, right now, here!" There's a lot of laughter. Water injects humor into even a special romantic dinner with silly playfulness that warms your heart, making you laugh so hard your wine will spray out of your mouth and nose! Water always pushes to do exciting and unpredictable things together.

Uh-Uh, Baby!

Water is uninhibited in the bedroom. While making love, their movement along with their touch gives a profound sense of connection. Peering intently into their lover's eyes, they connect from the depths of their bones. The bonding is completely wordless, but the eyes speak a thousand words. That much intense focus can be riveting and fulfilling for some and unnerving for others.

This type of connection isn't the heart-to-heart connection of Fire. It's also not Metal's ethereal and sublime connection. It's the kind of connection that involves a guttural grunt, like, "Uhhhhh! I want you now!" You don't think about it; you just feel the immediacy of your passion at a gut level. You need to do it *now*! Your bodies sense each other at the bone level, deep inside. The energy comes from the loins.

Having sex with Water for the first time might be a surprise after what we've just described. As they're getting to know you, they can be timid and have an awkward way of touching and moving. They hesitate a lot, watch you, and expect you to move. They are unsure of what you will do, and check it out. The starting might seem slow, and then it builds to a crescendo, a sexual tsunami in the Elemental world, as they feel safer and get drawn into the moment.

Drama, Trauma, and the Dalai Lama…

Drama is present more than ever in our culture due to television. Shows today create drama through entertainment competitions like *American Idol, The Voice,* and *Dancing with the Stars* as well as twenty-four-hour-news events accompanied by dramatic music and flashing graphics. Even sporting events are portrayed with theatrical flair detailing the athletes' personal lives. You can't escape the drama! So don't be surprised if your Water partner thinks quality time is on the couch watching TV with you.

Water *loves* the excitement of drama. In every conversation or activity, they create drama around them. Their voice ranges from talking excitedly in high tones to talking in deep, resonant tones that create a sense of gravity, urgency, momentum, or fear. They even may sit on the edge of their chair waiting, tapping their foot, ready to stand up super fast if they need to escape a room quickly. They're not looking for trouble. They're actually very chill, but they're innately ready for anything.

In his public talks, the most revered Water monk in the world, His Holiness the Dalai Lama, is far from somber. During a talk at MIT that we both attended, he playfully upstaged the more serious presenter who introduced him, by putting on an MIT baseball cap and hamming it up, making silly gestures with it. He then proceeded to tell story after story about the events in his life, all the people he met, what they wanted, and how he dealt with them. Water loves to tell a good story! They draw it out. They build a story slowly into a crescendo. It ramps up and then spills out rapidly. The Dalai Lama travels the world telling his stories and imparting his wisdom.

If your partner is Water, you might not appreciate their dramatic storytelling in every case. One woman called her husband from the emergency room and left a four-minute voice message describing what had happened. Her monotone droned on with her story, from beginning to end, leaving her partner to wonder up until the end of the voice message whether she had a splinter or a broken leg! She just went on and on and on. Cutting to the chase would have deprived her of all the fun and drama out of narrating her story. It ended up being something closer to the splinter, which made the voice message a great example of Water's tendency to be dramatic.

Because our society doesn't necessarily support Water's desire to be in constant motion or to be completely still, the thing Water wants most in life is permission to be wild, silly, and intense—preferably all three at once. Even better is to find someone to help amp up the intensity with.

Intensity is Water's driving force and reason to be alive. Intensity may take the form of complete silliness and almost hysterical laughter. Or it may be the drama over an injury or emergency, and the urgent need to respond immediately.

The original meaning of the word *drama* was "to do" or "to act." Doing theater and performing on a stage is a perfect outlet for all Water's dramatic energy. Can you stand all this drama? Water loves it, thrives on it, and seeks it out.

If your partner is Water, you may be surprised when suddenly they jump up from bed if there's any disturbance in the night, a clanking in the backyard, or a distant siren. Their heightened senses help them hear things you can't hear. And they respond immediately.

Stick in the Waterwheel

When Water falls in love, their natural sporadic rhythm and freedom may change. They are so amenable and follow others so easily that they often don't pay attention to themselves. So they can end up doing whatever their new partner wants them to do, going with the flow of their new love. This might end up confusing the new partner because they want their Water lover to do all the amazing things they have the potential to do. Instead, the Water partner might be very content to not move at all, especially if they're focusing on the partner or home life.

Sometimes they even experience a kind of depression. They don't really know they are depressed, but they haven't done the things they love to do in so long that they end up sitting around and doing nothing. Often the practicalities of life become overwhelming and they feel like they have to conform. They feel compelled to live predictable home lives, work a responsible job, and raise children. Then they might seem lazy and disinterested as if they've lost their drive.

One Water who has a relatively low-intensity job fills his need for drama with a constant stream of hobbies he does intensely. Over the past five years, he went from collecting motorcycles—soon filling his yard with motorcycle parts— to collecting wood for woodworking, filling his basement and garage completely with someday-to-be-used (his wife wonders when) planks of fine wood. Another woman bought and collected crafting supplies of every type—soon filling her house like a crafts store and then turning her attention to her green thumb, buying so many plants there is no room left for people in her home. Water needs these hobbies to make up for lack of excitement in their day-to-day life.

If the Water you fell in love with was adventurous and spontaneous but now is bogged down with career and responsibilities, you can initiate doing intense fun things to help your relationship flow again. Maybe start slow. Go for a hike, ride bikes, go jet skiing, attend comedy shows. If you have children or grandchildren, you can take the whole family to fairs, amusements parks, and other attractions. Water loves playing with children because they love to be silly and in the moment. This is a great way to get Water out of the house to play.

In Water We Trust

The Water Element's greatest virtue is trust. Water simply trusts that everything will work out okay. They are incredibly patient people. This is sometimes hard for a partner to watch because Water is very comfortable waiting for change. The people who love them often find themselves encouraging them to make changes, but their response is "Soon…all in good time." It's difficult to rush Water along when they don't want to rush.

Their patience is a great quality. They have an innate knowing when is the right time to move. They don't move too soon or too late. A partner who worries all the time, though, can disrupt this natural ability. If you're a worrier, your Water partner might get caught up in your concerns and stop trusting. If they lose their trust, they'll have a huge crisis for them, almost an identity crisis. This is one of Water's challenges.

When they lose their trust, they begin to be afraid of one possibility occurring. They think if they make the wrong move, it might cause something really bad to happen. This fear can be so great that they refuse to move at all, and they become a frozen pool until that possibility goes away. Sometimes Water can be frozen for years trying to avoid a particular outcome. Then they can live a stagnant life.

Low Tide

Water tends to take an inventory of their own energy. The Chinese call this our storehouse of energy. What gets spent must be replenished. They are constantly gauging their energy levels, like the ocean's tide cycles. If they don't have enough stored energy from eating and sleeping, they won't be able to do something intense when the situation arises. They inventory and monitor the flow of important resources in life, like their water (preventing dehydration), their cash (keeping extra on hand, they always have something stashed away and make great accountants), and their sleep and energy supplies (sleeping for a whole day after too much exertion).

Are You in Love with Water?

Water often has a look of alertness in their eyes even if they are quiet. They aren't afraid to start a conversation with a stranger. They have nothing to fear and will take you along for a fun ride if you let them. But how can you tell if your partner is Water? You can observe how your lover interacts with the world, through the eyes, the walk, and the sound of the voice. The way someone moves tells you about their Elemental Energy type.

The Walk: Skating Through Life

Waters hold all their power in their kidneys in their lower back. Imagine they have two giant jet engines inside their backs, and they're sitting on the tarmac waiting for takeoff.

When watching them walk, they actually accelerate suddenly, almost jerking forward in the rush. Their hips propel them forward faster than most. When they push their hips forward, picking their feet up very far becomes almost impossible. So they lift their feet only slightly off the ground, which makes them look like they're skating. They are not usually scuffing their feet, however, since scraping their shoes along the ground would slow them down. If your partner has the skating-on-ice walk, it's a clear sign that Water is in his or her top three Elements, probably your partner's first Element.

They tend to walk in two ways. When they're not in a hurry, they might have a slow-motion saunter. But they're not dawdling. Their pace can be relaxed like a slow-flowing stream. But more commonly, they walk in the second way, a purposeful and powerful, hurried walk. They look like they might even break into a run. Like a rushing river cutting its way through a canyon, they appear determined to get somewhere. Wood's walk may look similar but has different features. Wood's walk is direct and goal-oriented but doesn't look rushed or hurried. Waters push and propel themselves forward with whatever power they need. It's the forward force that distinguishes Water from Wood.

The Talk: Thisiswhatawaterperson sometimessoundslikewhentheytalk

The Water voice has two styles. The first vocal pattern is stop-and-start, almost hesitating and waiting. They anticipate the person they're speaking to might jump in at any moment. In this mode, it's almost a stutter step. Sometimes they don't even finish their sentences because they think of something else. In mid-sentence, they pause for a split second, and then, forgetting their first sentence, start a second train of thought. The second mode of speaking is the run-on sentence, which Water sometimes uses without stopping or pausing for punctuation. Although the voice is often monotone when it's in run-on sentence mode, its pitch can rise and fall quickly before becoming monotone again. Often it builds momentum to a crescendo, unable to stop, which can be quite dramatic, even shocking when sudden changes in volume occur. Sometimes the voice also builds suspense through drama and dramatic pauses. When the voice is high in this mode, it vibrates in the throat, making it sound like mild hysteria (don't be alarmed, Water is not hysterical, but quite calm, even when excited). When the voice is low, it has a gravely groaning sound that drones on and on.

The Look: Panoramic View

Water's eyes are intensely aware of their surroundings. When open wide, their eyes take in everything at once, even peripherally. When they are cat-like slits, they look like they don't trust the world, wary of any movement. Don't confuse Water's with Earth's big eyes; Earth's eyes are soft, wide-open, comforting, and doe-like, whereas, when Water's eyes are wide open, they're anything but soft, rather, they're buzzing with intensity as they take it all in.

What Does Water Want?

If you're Water, what you want most is to have a playmate who lets you be silly, spontaneous, and dramatic. Better yet, you want a lover who will share the excitement with you, where the fun can go on relentlessly, and then do nothing for long periods of time, without judgment! Out of all the couples who find partners who are the same Element, the most common is two Waters. They like to be with others who are like themselves because they can have so much fun together being crazy and silly, and they have just as much fun being lazy on the couch all day.

Although Water really just wants to share the way they are totally plugged into life with someone else, they don't need a lot of emotional connection. They simply love to have someone to do stuff with, laugh, and enjoy life. Water is the quirky, unpredictable, and fun Element.

The Evolution of Water

When Water is waiting for a partner to have fun with, they are relying on someone else to create the intensity in their lives. They could wait a lifetime, using the lack of love as an excuse to not do much and feel alone.

But as with any of the Five Elements, we all have to look inside for what we want from other people. With or without a lover, Water has to be plugged in to the energy stream of life. The idea that energy can only be generated by sleeping or resting is limiting because every Water has times when sleep is not an option. The Chinese believe that there is universal energy in the atmosphere, and some Waters learn to exist on less sleep, simply by taking in this "cosmic" energy. When they're taking energy from the cosmos, they can recover much faster from their intense, fun events.

We could say the life of Water should be the X-Life (as in extreme). When every day feels exciting, fresh, and energized simply because life is grand, then Water is living its fullest.

In order to live the X-Life, they need to be connected to their inner trust. We call this Trust with a capital T. They trust in their own safety and ability to know what to do in any given moment. When they have Trust, the search for a playmate and partner is no longer necessary. They trust the right people will join them on their many expeditions. And it's true because Water attracts people who want to have fun and laugh.

What is this Trust about? It's trusting the Divine Source of life. It's a deep connection with wisdom and knowing that goes beyond words and book learning. They offer the world this wisdom, like the coolest Water singer of our times, Bob Marley, when he sings his most popular song "One Love." It's the perfect Water song.

Flow forth, Water. May the force be with you.

Eight

Most Wanted

....

"Only you have the power to choose for yourself."

W. Clement Stone

....

Many people ask us which Element is the best. Ha! The answer is, all the Elements are amazing and fascinating in each person. Each Element has a different set of gifts and virtues. (But as a joke we tell the Woods they're the best because they're the Element that loves to be just a little bit better than the rest.)

It's totally fine if you identify with more than one Element. After you read this book, if you really think you're all five, try going with Water first. Almost all the people who tell us, "Well, I think I am all of them," usually end up being Water.

In an ideal world we would all be able to live and play in all of our Five Elements when needed. We would all burst forth in spring, mature in summer, give away and let go in the fall, hibernate in winter, and transition easily between all these phases. Yet, our constitution is such that we manifest one of the Elements more strongly than all the others throughout our lives. We can't help it.

What's really important here is to figure out which Element is your true nature so that you know how to be your authentic self. Then you can figure out what your partner's Element is. Or if you're looking for a new relationship, read chapter ten to help you decide what Elemental energy you want to draw into your life at this very moment. You can, from the very start of the relationship, celebrate your new love's best qualities, while realizing that the things you don't like about them are actually normal, instead of bad and wrong. When your partner expects (or demands) you to be someone you're not, you can also explain why your strengths and weaknesses are normal and supposed to be different from theirs. Sometimes it takes courage to be yourself, even with the one you love.

You Want What?

As a couple moves beyond the initial and very exciting honeymoon stage into a more serious long-term relationship, eventually they must each ask what they really want. Wow, what a concept to actually talk about these things together *before* they get too deep into a relationship. Here are a few examples:

- If you are Wood, you want someone to truly see how great you are. Personally, you don't even want to think about your faults or bad habits. If your lover tells you, "You messed up, but I love you anyway," that is the complete opposite of what you want to hear. You don't like to ever mess up or be criticized. You always wants to hear all the good reasons why you're loved.

- If you are Fire, you want unconditional love. This means you want someone to love all your faults, not just the best parts of you. You want to know that no matter how badly you screw up that your lover will still love you. You also want to feel beautiful and be adored (all the time).

- If you are Earth, you want to be understood. You want your lover to "get" you on a deep, deep level. If your lover understands that all the difficulties you've encountered have made you a better person, then they might be able to relate to you. Understanding has to be expressed in words... lots (and lots) of words. You want to hear your partner say something that validates your exact emotional state at the time.

- If you are Metal, you want your lover to love you with a cosmic connection. It's as if you connect with the entire cosmos through your lover. Communication requires very little talking when you've connected this way. There is a deep sense of honoring and respect that comes with this kind of love.

It's a meaningful touch with no words and a deep eye gaze that says a thousand words. Sublime.

- If you are Water, you want love that reaches the depths beyond the words of our language. Normal surface conversations are boring. It's diving deep down, communicating without words, but with a power and intensity of movement and sharing, producing alternating calm and activity that makes life exciting.

Why Can't You Be More Like... (Insert Name Here)?

We realize all this talk of knowing what you want and being yourself isn't easy for everyone. Sometimes children are born to parents who are completely opposite of them energetically. The parents naturally want their children to behave just like them. "You're being too loud." "Why can't you just sit still?" "Stop tapping your foot!" "Why do you have to *always* be right?" "Slow down!" So the message those children receive from the get-go is, "Don't be like you ... Be like me!" It's natural that a child tries to emulate parental behaviors. It's also natural to feel like you don't fit in if you don't behave or feel like your parents. If this was your experience growing up or your partner's, awareness is the first step to resolving past issues.

When this is the case, often those children default to their second Element or sometimes their third Element on a day-to-day basis to fit into the family. They essentially try to become like their parents, which never bodes well for the child, especially after growing up and entering the adult world. They're living inauthentically. They are often very lost in themselves, not clear who they are, and feeling ashamed to be their true selves. These people might spend fifty percent of their time in their second Element until they learn how to be more authentic.

Elemental Road Blocks

Often, no matter what Element you are, your energy gets blocked and it can be difficult to be fully present. You end up living life in your second or third Element over time. This can even hinder your sex drive. Your libido is on snooze and nothing seems to be able to wake it up. Sure you could point fingers at your partner, parents, siblings, children, or a stressful event in your life, but basically nothing is putting you in the mood for anything. When you experience this kind of indifference, it typically means your energy is blocked. Following are some examples.

Wood-a, Could-a, Should-a

When Wood loves life, you are springing forward, full of enthusiasm and playfulness, wanting to discover new (sexual) situations on a regular basis. Wood partners often show their soft side after a lovemaking workout. They delight in satisfying their partners, often putting them first, but making sure they save enough energy for both parties to be happy (wink, wink). A happy Wood lover means everyone is happy! Wood's win-win strategy in life almost always follows into the bedroom.

When your energy is blocked, you're probably obstructed in life if you are not able to do what you want in your career or some personal goal you have. You're angry or depressed. You might even get really mean.

Solution: You have to identify your obstacles before you can overcome them. Invent a new game to clear your way through it. Looking at the bigger picture in your life may offer some help. It can be especially challenging for Wood, but sometimes you have to cut things loose, even though you have invested a lot of time and energy in them.

Kiss My Ashes

When Fire is in love with life (and themselves), they have an open heart. They put themselves out there into the world with passion. They are funny, effervescent, and loving life like sparkling champagne in a just-opened bottle. Pop!

Fires can have huge appetites for sex. If you find the right partner, you two can enjoy a never-ending buffet of sexual delights. If your partner is Fire and happy with life, you may have to say *no* once in a while. Otherwise you may not have a life outside the bedroom!

As Fire, when your energy is blocked, you're probably unhappy with your body, feeling unattractive, disliked, insecure, and down on yourself. This is a big block.

Solution: Take a few weeks to focus completely on your inner and outer beauty. Wake up every day with the intention of doing something to feel better about how you look and feel in your body. Buy new clothes, get your hair done, join a gym, meditate...whatever it takes until you feel like you're rocking your inner and outer beauty again.

Downed to Earth

When Earth is in love with life, you're sharing deeply with a partner all the incredible, amazing events and realizations of your day. Sexually, you give so much so freely and happily when you feel a part of a wonderful exchange and a sense of reciprocity. You love to take turns giving and receiving. When Earth is happy, you feel like your partner is cherishing and nourishing you. Enjoying a wonderful meal or dessert can be very fulfilling. Sharing time and food together with a special person can make everything feel right. It's more than the sex you're enjoying; the whole ambiance and experience of a romantic night of sharing time and space with no separation is what's special. It's like you are two beings merging together and sharing life's bounty. It's okay when you give more than you receive. As Earth, you might be the more dominant lover when you feel totally connected and merged with your lover. In life, you share ideas and thoughts with community and friends. You can find many new things to create each and every day.

When Earth energy is blocked, you're likely bored with life and just going through the motions. Maybe you've been serving everyone else and not serving yourself, pun intended. This may even cause you to be mean or overly worried.

Solution: It's time to do something for yourself. Get out and find your community. Maybe join (or start) a new class. Go out and do *something*, anything social. Or maybe the block stems from your perception that your partner is not pulling their weight in the relationship. It's time for a talk to restore balance in the relationship. The most common reason for Earth to withhold sex is the feeling that you're doing everything and your partner is just skating along.

Heavy Metal

When Metal is in love with life, there is so much movement— meeting with friends, being outdoors, making love for hours (and hours), eating wonderful food with someone you truly care about. Life is a sensual and tactile delight of life. Sex is a slow, sensory experience. It's about just being suspended in time and space and feeling your body. Touch, smell, texture— all filling you with a beautiful sense of cosmic connection.

When Metal energy is blocked, you can feel dark and heavy. You feel you've sacrificed so much for everyone else. You may feel like you're not getting any credit for the enormous amounts of effort and work you're putting into relationships. Maybe you feel like you're not getting anywhere, spinning your wheels. This wears a person down over time and depression can set in. You may ask, "Why bother?"

Solution: It's time to give yourself what you crave and pat yourself on the back for all the good you do in the world.

Then move on, find a new endeavor. Really commit to some task you have been putting off. Make new connections and break out of your social isolation. Let the wind take you to a new fresh place, and your whole life, including your sex life, will slide back in as soon as you move on to new thoughts, ideas, and ventures.

Dam It

When Water is in love with life, anything is possible, and you're ready for it. You're anticipating awesome fun things to happen at every moment. You don't mind waiting for the good stuff. You're excited, well-rested, and gathering energy as you move through life. You are full of so much energy that your sexual encounters are explosions of life and deep connections with incredible endurance. You love being romantic.

If you're blocked, it is like you are a frozen pond in deep winter. There's not much going on in your life; you are so stuck! This almost always happens because you're afraid of some outcome, and it's easier to limit your life to barely any movement. This will ensure that the feared outcome will never arrive.

You don't feel sexual in this place even though you continue to have sex since you're not doing anything else. Still, it's as if you're afraid to be intense or the ice will melt, and the things you want to avoid might come back with even more force.

Solution: The only way out of this block is to face your fears. Sometimes this requires some introspection because sometimes you don't even know what you're afraid of because the fear is so strong you're avoiding thinking about it. Once you determine what has got you frozen, it's time to face the fear with the belief that you will know what to do if that outcome ever did arise. That is the Water way. You always know what to do. It just comes to you in the moment. You need to resume living in the now moment, getting into the flow and trusting your inner wisdom again.

What Are My Partner's Elements?

Discovering your Element is just one half of the equation. Of course, the most important question is: what Element is my lover?

We always recommend watching your partner walk and listening to the sound of their voice. And remember that as you're learning about Elemental Energy, you also need to use your common sense.

One basic way to understand the Elements in people is to think about how they engage. What types of interactions do they have with other people in the world—at their job, at the grocery store, at a restaurant? What are they trying to achieve in their conversations? How is your partner or lover trying to interact with you? Sometimes just watching them converse with someone, you can start to see the energy behind everything they do.

Wood Engages

Wood wants to get a reaction from people. They're having fun and want to find people who are aware and awake enough to notice. They love to see how quickly you can respond to their fast thinking and quick wit. Can you be so on it that you know what to say before the words leave the other person's mouth? Wood can! They are quick-witted, and they know almost instantly when they meet another Wood. They love to find someone who can challenge them on a regular basis, who pushes them to be smarter, funnier, faster... better than ever.

Fire Connects with the Heart

Fire actually feels connections in the heart. When their partner is closed off and connecting only with their head and not their heart, Fire can *feel* it. They can quickly come undone if they feel disconnected on that deep heart level. Heart-to-heart interaction is based on engaging your emotions, which go beyond the logical mind. You wear your heart on your sleeve, put yourself out there, to find someone who is willing to connect with an open heart for moments or a lifetime.

Earth Is a Mind Meld

This is the ability to talk and talk and talk. To mull, break down, and digest thoughts together. To turn them around and around and look at them from all angles and then come down to the root problems, thereby figuring out the answers together. Mind melding is a process that requires thought and words, but in a sexual setting can be about mind melding through touch and a conversation through bodies. I do something, now it's your turn to talk and "say" something back through the quality of your touch. Then it's my turn again.

Metal Opens Cosmic Space

Metal feels the fullness of this connection in their chest, like taking a deep breath inward. It feels sacred. Sexual intimacy is always the ultimate connection through touch and the senses. Sexually the time and space you share becomes precious. Your bodies are sacred temples of worship with sexual energy running all the time. You share that together and feel overwhelmed by the sublime beauty of your connection.

Water Is Intense Sharing

You feel intensity through a depth of connection that's wordless but full of power. You feel the power deep down in your body, especially when having sex. The groin area is the center of your power zone. Intensity through fun and silliness can even be found in the bedroom! Spontaneity and unpredictability makes Water a passionate and fun-loving Element. Water connects urgently with a quickening, an intense movement, and a search for each other's souls.

Seek and You Shall Find

Knowing what you really want in a relationship is the key to success. How can you expect to find that person who excites you, who fills you with pure joy, or who finally "gets" you in a way that feels amazing and true, if you don't get who *you* are yourself and what you want? How can you expect your partner to love your gifts and virtues if you're doing everything you can to hide them? Self-acceptance is key. Embrace your Element and learn to rock it!

You may want someone who is totally engaged and sees you for all the good you do (Wood). Or you may be motivated by seeking unconditional love (Fire). Or you may want to find someone who truly gets you (Earth). You may want a sense of connection that is cosmic and sublime (Metal). Or another type of connection that is deep and intense (Water).

Are you willing to accept yourself and accept your partner the way you both are? It requires knowing who you both are, accepting your differences, even loving your differences. Because together, as a team, you are much stronger than the individual parts if you learn how to leverage the best of what each of you has to offer.

Nine

Making Love Connections

....

"Love is our true destiny. We do not find the meaning
of life by ourselves alone—we find it with another."

Thomas Merton

....

Now that you've been introduced to the Five Elements and
all their wonderful facets, you should know or be close to
identifying your Element. If you currently have a partner or
a romantic interest, you may have tried to figure out that
person's Element. Let's explore the dynamics of the different
kinds of Elemental relationships. Feel free to use this chapter
as a reference, skipping directly to the sections and charts
that pertain to you for now. Then later you can give it a full

reading if you desire. Who knows? This might even help you win an occasional argument with your lover. We're kidding—it's not really about winning at all but about creating greater compromise and acceptance in your relationship.

But first, here's a general explanation that everyone needs to understand.

This book is really about connections … making connections within yourself and with others. As we make connections, we are mostly unconscious about the effect our energy has on others. But we can become self-aware and utilize our energy to everyone's benefit. This is not manipulation, or trying to make someone do something. On the contrary, it's a way to get along better and be more connected to those we love than ever before. All your relationships will take on new meanings once you learn how Elemental Energies interact with each other.

Same, Nourishing, or Controlling: Your Energy Dynamic

Energy interactions have three different types of relationships—same, nourishing, and controlling. Whatever your Elemental Energy type, you will have a particular type of reaction to another person based on whether their energy type is the same as yours or different. If different, you can figure out whether it feeds your energy or attempts to control it.

Same: Just Like Me

Have you ever met someone who instantly makes you feel at home? They are so much like you that it just feels easy. You speak the same language. You have the same sense of humor. You have similar gestures. Even if you come from opposites ends of the world, you sense that you could be best friends despite hardly knowing each other yet. You both have the same energy signature and are the same Elements. Who doesn't like loving themselves? This is the gift of the Same/Same Energy dynamic.

Or at times you meet certain people just like you but they irritate you! What? Yep, you're looking in the mirror but maybe not liking what you see. They do the same things you do, but instead of appreciating that sameness, you feel put off or even nauseated as you realize that is what you do too! Sometimes meeting your alter ego brings out the critic in you. Maybe you thought you'd overcome a negative trait you see in the other person. But that person reminds you of what you had disliked in yourself. You desperately wish they'd stop before someone else sees how foolish they're being. It's an embarrassment that they don't get it. This is the downside of the Same/Same Energy dynamic.

Nourishing: The Parent Trap

In order to survive and thrive as infants, all human beings on this planet need to be held, fed, soothed, and have someone make them feel safe. These are basic, fundamental needs. We can add in clothing and cleanliness too. As we grow, we may gain independence from our parents, but we still always love that nourishing energy. This is true for everyone. It is a human instinct, strong in some, weaker in others. Often times, we seek out the Element that fulfills needs through friendship or in our romantic lives.

Sometimes we feel hungry and deprived. We have certain unmet needs. Maybe we didn't have that kind of nourishment as babies. Or maybe we've spent half our lives being the one in charge, the giving one, and we just want someone who will take care of us for a change.

Whatever the reason, we feel comfortable when we're with the people who are our natural caretakers. Caretakers also enjoy the company of those who appreciate all they have to offer. It is a symbiotic relationship that can be very rewarding for both involved.

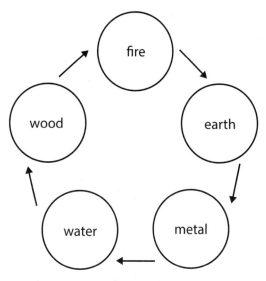

Figure 2: Nourishing Cycle Relationships

Nourishing Cycle Relationships		
Wood	fuels	Fire
Fire	warms	Earth
Earth	produces	Metal
Metal	contains	Water
Water	feeds	Wood

These relationships are always fairly easy. The only time they run into trouble is when the parent Element gets tired of being the one who always gives. If the parent Element is unwell or upset and cuts off the nourishment, the child

Element panics. This characterization sounds dramatic, and but usually it's so subtle that most of us don't even realized that it's going on. For example, let's say you are the one in the parenting role, nourishing a lover. You've always been there for the other person. But suddenly you're struggling yourself from a sudden illness, loss of job, or something as simple as the drama of a speeding ticket on the ride home. Your energy has dissipated, and you just don't have a lot left to give. Your partner sees that you're struggling and immediately feels very uneasy. They may have come to rely on your strength. You may want a sympathetic ear, but your partner can't really be present for you. They want you to feel better as soon as possible. They just want to fix the problem and offer a whole list of suggestions. Or they might disappear into the backyard, unable to be supportive. Or they might ask your best friend to come help. They just want to restore the balance in your relationship so they can continue to receive the nourishment you usually give freely.

The other time a nourishing relationship can struggle is when the child Element gets rebellious or feels uneasy and tries to out-parent the parent. They become insubordinate and resent the parent Element always telling them what to do, suddenly rejecting all the nourishment they were taking in. Then they assert their energetic independence like a defiant teenager.

Controlling: Push My Buttons, Please

Sometimes the people you are most attracted to are the most opposite of you. Is life a little boring? Maybe you want to spice things up. What better way than to find someone who's your opposite. Opposites attract, right? You want to know more. Think of visiting a foreign country. It's different from what you're used to. You want to know everything about the people, learn to speak the language, experience eating the food. It's an exciting change from your way of life, and for a time, you love the difference.

In an opposite relationship, one Element controls another. No matter what type of person you are, even if you're the most powerful outgoing person you know, there is someone you bow to energetically. But control's not always a bad thing in a relationship. It creates a lot of sexual tension and excitement. Some people thrive on it. Some people hate it.

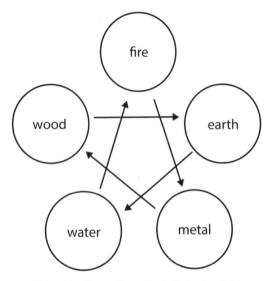

Figure 3: Controlling Cycle Relationships

Controlling Cycle Relationships		
Wood	breaks up	Earth
Fire	melts	Metal
Earth	dams	Water
Metal	chops	Wood
Water	extinguishes	Fire

Just the other day, a man was bragging to how easy it is for him to make things happen in the world. He's confident, he's assertive, and he's a mover and shaker. Pop quiz! What Element do you think he is? This is a test…if you guessed Wood, you're right.

After a little boasting about his amazing life, this Wood sheepishly says, "Well, there is one thing I'd like help with. I experience a bizarre performance anxiety when the leader of my drumming circle asks me to play. The strange thing is I don't have performance anxiety in any other part of my life, ever, and I talk to people for a living." What was confusing to him is that he goes every week to this class and he loves it. Why would he have this reaction?

The reason is much simpler than he thought. His leader is Metal. Metal is the only Element who can make Wood feel small. What cuts down a tree? Metal! Metal is the Elemental Energy signature that can bring Woods to their knees and also get them to do things they may not like or enjoy.

Now imagine this in a romantic relationship. In one way, Wood might like to have someone who controls them in their bedroom since they're in charge everywhere else. It might be a relief to give up the reins. In fact, the attraction of opposites can produce very powerful sexual energy. But on another level, no one wants to have performance anxiety in the bedroom. Talk about sexual dysfunction.

Now, that same Wood who is awkward and shy with a Metal person, is a total bossy pants when Earths are around! Wood controls Earth by trying to make them move faster, make quicker decisions, and act more intuitively before thinking things over. Earth wants to take their time to analyze and evaluate everything—all the time. Earth can't really keep up with Wood energetically and gets somewhat flustered when Wood assigns them tasks and wants them done right away. So in a romantic relationship, they need to find the balance, the give and take that makes the relationship exciting and beneficial.

Tie Me Up, Tie Me Down

Maybe at times you've scared yourself. When you allow yourself to fully be yourself, yikes! You are too much. You might even feel embarrassed. Then you might feel that you'd like to get better control of parts of yourself and live a different kind of life. If you really let yourself live to your full potential without restraints, who knows what might happen? Maybe you'll get hurt or hurt someone else emotionally.

So what do you do? You seek out that opposite energy, someone who will tame you, bring you back into the social mainstream. Someone who will guide you and say, "No, we don't really behave like that. Watch me. Do it like me." And instead of feeling angry about not being allowed to be yourself, you're relieved because you don't have to push yourself. You don't have to manifest your huge potential. You can be small, unassuming, and blend in. Your partner helps tether you down from flying out of control.

The Control Officer

The problem with any Controlling Relationship is that the person being controlled can resent the subordinate role and revolt. But resistance has its price. By asserting independence, the controlling partner almost always feels insulted.

In other words, the controlled Element has to be mean to regain control. They rise up against the controlling Element, get angry and fight back. This dynamic, called the Insulting Cycle in Chinese Five Element theory, can be the root cause of why some couples bicker back and forth. This type of relationship can get very ugly when the Controlled Element seizes control back. But don't worry, there is a way to coexist.

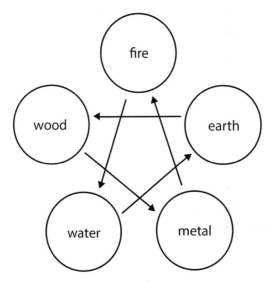

Figure 4: Insulting Cycle

Labor of Love

If you're starting a new relationship or discovering the Element of your long-time partner, one of the first things you can look at is how you divide up the daily tasks of life. Often people gravitate to doing the things that are easy for their

Elemental Energy type. This will help reveal which type of relationship you have.

Take something as simple as when you first move in together as a couple. There's this whole dance that goes on in the beginning. Let's call it the *Division of Labor,* such as, who is going to take out the trash, do the dishes, manage the household bills, make the social arrangements with friends, put together the furniture, make important calls, etc. In a relationship, there are certain tasks that go really well with certain Elements. These are all gender-neutral roles. It is about the energy matrix and the Element matrix of each person, *not* their gender. Here are some examples of the Division of Labor in action.

Let's say you and your partner want to rent an apartment together. One person is Wood and one person is Fire. The one who is Fire is chattier and can be in charge of calling and scheduling the meetings with landlords. The rent and lease negotiations require a more assertive nature, which is easy for Wood. They are good negotiators and a win-win scenario would be great.

Both the Wood and Fire can be good at meeting and greeting the neighbors. The one who is Fire may be a good choice for setting up all the new billing accounts, arranging for address changes and handling the paperwork stuff that Wood usually hates! The one who is Wood can take charge of the neatness brigade, since Fire is often a bit more scattered on that front. Or better yet, Wood could hire someone to help clean up. Trying to get partners to do something they're not good at or hate doing is never wise. Look at the strengths and challenges of Wood and Fire and a dynamic couple will emerge!

If Water and Earth are in a romantic relationship, who would be the best person to take care of all the couple's social plans? Earth is more social. Who would plan the yearly vacations? Actually both Water and Earth love to travel, so it could be a shared task. The one who is Earth might be best at putting together the things that arrive in boxes since Earth will actually read the instructions and take the time to meticulously go through them. People who are Earth excel at reading manuals, instruction booklets, and informational labels. Heck, they're the ones who write them! They get the small stuff. They get it—they don't sweat it!

What Is Your Relationship Dynamic?

The rest of this chapter provides you with specifics about each Elemental Energy type. If you've figured out you and your partner's Elements, you can look up your Elemental dynamics together. If you're looking for a new love in your life, you will want to read your Element in combination with the other four elements. Maybe you will see something that strikes your fancy.

Relationship Dynamics					
Wood/Wood	168	Wood/Fire	174	Wood/Earth	182
Fire/Fire	169	Fire/Earth	175	Fire/Metal	185
Earth/Earth	171	Earth/Metal	177	Earth/Water	186
Metal/Metal	172	Metal/Water	179	Metal/Wood	188
Water/Water	173	Water/Wood	180	Water/Fire	190

Same/Same Relationships: To Know Me Is to Love Me

Wood/Wood: Knock on Wood

Wood has charisma and charm and likes to be in charge, even in the bedroom.

When two Woods meet, the big question is, "What's the chain of command?" Right away they start a sort of dance, an unspoken posturing in which they're both subtly trying to figure out who is the bigger Wood. Both have to work out who's in charge. It's also possible that the power might swing back and forth between them. It's not sexual, it's energetic. So as lovers, you might really admire each other greatly. Who else does as good a job as you do in the world? It's amazing to find a co-captain for the A-team.

Even in bed, if you're Wood, you might allow your partner to think they're "on top" or in charge, but you've quietly orchestrated everything. This doesn't mean you're orchestrating sex to benefit you alone. In fact, you're probably working just as hard to make sex work for your partner as much as for your own satisfaction.

In life, it can be difficult for two Wood partners to negotiate the day-to-day life with each other. You both want to be the general and commander, so to speak. Having two bosses and no underlings makes for a difficult, sometimes competitive household. Who's going to do all the little things if both people are tending to the big vision? A Wood/Wood couple is going to need a support system.

In theory, you'll both feel for the first time in life you've met your match, and that's a really good feeling—it can be lonely at the top being the biggest and best all the time. It can be a relief to finally meet and fall in love with someone who is a bit bigger and better than you are. You don't have to carry the responsibility of being the biggest person all the time.

We know Wood/Wood couples exist, but it's the rarest of the Elemental matches we've encountered. To get the Wood win-win scenario will take a lot of work and patience, plus a support system. You'll either drive each other to excellence or off a cliff! Snarky, but true.

Fire/Fire: Mutual Admiration Society

Fire often gravitates to other Fires like moths to a flame—a party flame, that is! You like to have parties and social gatherings where there's a lot of laughter and storytelling. It's double the fun, double the parties, and double the friends.

Together, you also have double the passion in bed, right? Well, yes. Fires are the most passionate of all Elements. And you also love to have sex a lot, as often as possible in fact. Even if you don't have time to have sex, you're both thinking about it. So you can imagine if—wait, we'll just let you use *your* imagination and leave it at that! Whew, it's getting hot here!

Together, you have more than just great sex. The intimacy potential is off the charts because you can both be extremely openhearted and authentic. Then Fire/Fire couples are very long lasting and maintain an active sex life for many years, even decades.

Of course, just like anyone else, even a Fire couple's sexual stamina in sex can dwindle as the relationship matures. Intimacy problems, stemming from hurt feelings, will likely reduce the amount of sex they have in a week.

Fire loves to be attractive and desirable. When you are a Fire/Fire couple, who does the attracting and who is attracted? The answer is both. You have to take turns holding the mirror up to each other. Each of you showers attention on the other person. You both will delight in the attention you receive. Creating a Mutual Admiration Society together is the key to giving your partner the love and attention needed. Now, go on and tell each other how hot you *both* are.

But because you're both sensitive and can get your feelings hurt easily, there's twice as much potential for misunderstandings. A new Fire/Fire relationship might crash and burn quickly if sensitive feelings get hurt too often. But luckily for you, you both know how to communicate with your shut-down partner, since you know how it feels to get hurt. You can help your hurt lover feel better.

Like the phoenix rising from the ashes, Fire/Fire couples can come back stronger than ever. When your lover's heart opens back up again, expect a lot of tears. But they're good tears... tears of relief for love is returned. Once you both realize that the other person isn't going away, you can relax into a deeper commitment to each other.

Earth/Earth: Friends Without Benefits

Earth is often in search of that person who truly *gets* them. They want someone who meets them at the level of thought and heart (the Chinese call it heart/mind) that they require. How many times have you wished your whole life for someone to understand how you feel or to support you when you need help? Finally, to have a partner who does that, it's unbelievable! But... as with all Same/Same Element relationships, it has its challenges.

Earth is rarely sexually attracted to other Earths. It doesn't mean they're not amazing companions; many long-term relationships get built on this foundation, where sex is not as important. If you're Earth and looking to have amazing fulfilling sex with your Earth lover, you may feel as if you're trying to move mountains in the bedroom. For many Earths, their Earth/Earth romance can be tragic when they realize that this awesome new Earth romantic interest just doesn't light their fire, since they genuinely like this new partner and they get along so well.

That said, if you find an Earth person you are attracted to sexually, grab that person and hold on tight. Because they could totally rock your world. When the spark of passion is present, you have the potential for having it all—incredible sex and loyal companionship.

Earth is strong but incredibly giving. To meet someone who is as strong as you are, who can take turns equally in giving and receiving, and who understands what you like … well, that's just heaven on Earth.

Metal/Metal: Rockstar Lovers

A Metal/Metal combination is more common than most Same/Same Elemental relationships because of their compatibility. They can hang out together and not push each other to be more involved or go out or make things happen. You can chill together and just be.

The sex for a Metal/Metal couple can be off-the-charts amazing. They can spend hours and hours and hours making love. Starting at a slow pace, they allow each other to fully experience everything they're doing without rushing. Occupying a place where time does not exist, they just are, together, for as long as their lovemaking lasts. All their senses are fulfilled as they explore their senses together over and over. They can be serious or simply play. And when they're not playing, they're connecting deeply. They can feel totally within a spiritual moment, something greater than life. Through this cosmic connection they transcend the daily, humdrum routine of existence.

The world is constantly trying to get Metal to be people they aren't. They want you to talk more, be more engaged, do more. But with a Metal partner, you get approval for just hanging out. The challenge with Metal/Metal is that one Metal has to be assertive enough to actually pursue the other person. Often Metal ends up with other Elements who pursue them. Metal can sometimes end up romantically with whoever is energetically stronger and able to grab on to them tightly enough.

Water/Water: A River Runs Through It

Water/Water makes a good match. You both love having a playmate to do stuff with, whether it's sitting on the couch in front of the TV, rapelling down a waterfall, or swimming with the dolphins. You are really looking for someone to share intensity on many different levels. You don't have a lot of complicated emotional needs. So really, finding your Water lover makes a great match emotionally and physically.

Waters have a quirky sense of humor and love to laugh. It's great to have a partner who shares Water's style of humor. You both know that safety is important. While you enjoy doing things that feel daring and different, you won't push each other into taking risks that make you feel unsafe.

You also both love the drama of stimulating sex. There is a pulsating current that runs through Water/Water relationships. It's electrifying! This sexual attraction makes for intensity and lots of silliness in the bedroom. But the compatibility doesn't just stop there. Afterwards, you get to cuddle and snuggle for as long as you want, recuperating from your dramatic rendezvous.

The potential challenge to some Water/Water couples is that one partner might be the slower pooling kind of Water and the other might be the faster rushing kind of river. The faster one might flood the slower one with intensity, creating overload. One needs a lot more recovery and down time than the other and may end up exhausted after a time.

Nourishing Relationships: Round Peg, Round Hole
Wood/Fire: Power Playmates

Wood/Fire is a power couple relationship because they are both full of outward energy, fully engaged with the world.

For Wood, the relationship works because Fire is usually completely enamored of Wood, which totally makes Wood stand tall and feel great. So often Wood is taken for granted in the world and feels unappreciated for all the amazing things they do. Just because Wood does everything so easily does not mean that they want to go unnoticed or unseen. *Fire sees Wood's greatness.*

Fire is totally smitten with Wood's charisma. Fire loves people who are big in the world in the way they want to be but are often too shy to reveal. For Fire, the relationship works because Fire loves Wood's encouragement, cheerleading, and focus. Wood pays attention to Fire. In turn Fire loves that Wood finds them beautiful. It gives Fire confidence. Fire has so much love to give, but their shyness often gets in the way. They need to go out in the world every day feeling that they're loved (and look great). With Wood backing them, Fire feels safer about burning brightly for others to see. *Wood fuels Fire's passion.*

Sexually, Wood and Fire heat things up. The athleticism of Wood matching the passion of Fire can lead to a bonfire of sexual delights. This might mean a lot of strenuous activity. But Fire is totally up for the challenge because they love the attention Wood showers on them. Wood loves to be engaged in the heat of the moment.

While Wood and Fire are very compatible, there are a few differences that might present challenges. Wood's impatience and frustration about some general day-to-day life issues can lead to Fire's feelings getting hurt. Fire has to let this frustration pass (which it should quickly) without taking it personally.

Although focused on Wood's general needs, Fire often talks about themselves too much. Wood likes to know Fire is paying attention to their needs, too. Both enjoy being the center of attention and have to balance when each gets the focus. In general, humility and a sense of humor about their mutual desire for attention eases any tension in this area. The best way for Wood/Fire to succeed as a power couple is to keep stoking each other's fires with humor, openness, and sharing laughter.

Fire/Earth: Social Butterflies

Fire and Earth are the most social Elements. Fire/Earth is a very easy pairing because they talk and talk and talk—about everything!

Fire loves an audience, and what better listener is there than Earth? Earth is so attentive and listens so well. Fire feels safe and loved. Earth helps Fire be grounded and contained, like a fire circle. *Earth tends Fire.*

Earth loves to receive all the warmth Fire can give. Earth can feel very excited and animated around their Fire lover, almost like a giggly teenager. It feels really great to have a joyful Fire focused on them, enjoying them, and sharing fun things with them. Earth wants to be heard. They need someone to talk to about their problems. Fire loves to help Earth through the rough times and are very attentive and loving. Fire makes Earth feel really special and appreciated. It makes Earth's life feel more abundant and full. *Fire warms Earth's core.* Talking and listening, giving and receiving—see what a good match it is?

The sexual Fire/Earth combination is like a slow burn. It's not as big and animated as the Wood/Fire relationship, but a Fire/Earth romance is still very sexy and powerful. Earth brings the level of passion down to a smolder. They are very sure of their ability to satisfy their lover and can sometimes take control during lovemaking.

Earth loves when Fire listens. But Fire likes to find common ground and talk about things both partners are interested in so they can create a heart connection together. Earth enjoys taking turns when talking, and they respect differences of opinion. Fire/Earth couples need to allow each other the freedom to talk about whatever they want.

Earth can be very vocal when disappointed with Fire, which is like throwing a wet blanket on Fire's self-esteem. The challenge for this couple is that Earth always remembers what happened in the past, and Fire needs to know that it's been forgiven *and* forgotten. Past events can haunt a Fire/Earth couple for years unless they can get past it.

In the bedroom, when Fire and Earth take turns giving and receiving, Fire might lose its passion entirely. Fires are used to giving and receiving simultaneously, and they might (or might not) enjoy taking turns. Or Fires might feel they can't keep up with Earth's strength. Earth is steady and takes over, like a force of nature, throwing dirt on the flames. The challenge for Fire is not to feel inadequate in the face of this force. For long-term success, this easy-going couple needs to allow Fire to keep the passion in play. For example, the Earth lover may learn a faster pace in lovemaking or begin to give and receive at the same time.

Earth/Metal: Senses and Sensibilities

Earth is about giving, and Metal is about service. They are similar in their selfless desire to help others. They live to help others in the world. They make a good team, and they both love their home life, puttering around the house together.

Earth loves Metal's quiet attentiveness. Metal's presence is very soothing to have around like a safety net. Metal makes Earth feel rock solid. Earths loves that they can ask Metals to do projects for them. Metal is happy to serve. It makes Earth feel special. *Metal protects Earth.*

For Metal, Earth has so much to give. Earth takes care of so many things, cooking, cleaning, and following up on business matters. Most importantly, Earth handles all the social communications, which is a huge relief for Metal. There is a solidity to Earth that helps Metal feel safe and at home. *Earth makes Metal strong.*

Sometimes Earth and Metal clash—literally. Earth likes to harvest the bounty and give it away, feeling abundant and prosperous. Metal likes to conserve and save, cherishing what's most important. This fundamental difference can present a challenge for the couple.

In the bedroom, Earth's sensuality and Metal's focus on senses blend wonderfully together. Both Earth and Metal take turns, focus on sensations, and are slow. Their lovemaking can reach a real depth of spiritual connection in this couple's lovemaking. Earth with their understanding and caring, feeling into the other person's preferences. And Metal with their cosmic pure connection of unconditional love.

Metal can be a bit more experimental with their sexual desires than the Earth. Metal wants to really explore lots of scenarios and try new things. Earth is more focused on emotions and feelings. Earth is not really into the sexual experience alone. They want to please their lover in simple yet skilled ways. The desire to explore the physical realm might be difficult for Earth. But if Earth and Metal meet on sacred ground, then all will be well in the Earth/Metal realm. This may require Metal to focus on exploring the spiritual connection more than all the physical nuances of sensations. Earth is going to be much more willing to go the distance connecting on a higher plane.

Metal/Water: Liquid Metal

Metal and Water people share quietness, peacefulness, and focus on meditation. Through this focus, wisdom grows. The Metal sustains the Water, which needs to spend a lot of time relaxing and being quiet to reenergize after expending a lot of intense energy. It's so easy to be chill hanging with Metal. Like a sacred bowl, *Metal holds Water.*

Metal likes relaxing with Water, especially because Water isn't too chatty. When they do things together, they can be silent and yet still communicate with each other. But what Metal really likes about Water is that they enjoy nature and travel. Water is exciting at times for Metal, bringing new adventures that Metal might not normally seek out. *Water charges Metal.*

Metal's quiet attentiveness sometimes causes Water to be more erratic and unpredictable. Water likes to play the clown for Metal's amusement. When this happens, the two can be quite happy laughing hysterically all the time. However, Water can get carried away in the amount of noise and raucous they make. These unpredictable noises can be very jarring for some Metal's sensibilities. In general, whenever this happens Metal might startle and jump, feeling disturbed, even getting angry. Water needs to be aware of Metal's sensitive side.

Metal is organized and likes to put things in their proper place. Water is disorganized and lets things spill out all over the place. Metal doesn't like to clean much, so the two together could be quite messy. This may be fine for Water, but it continuously causes Metal grief.

In the bedroom, the Water/Metal combination is very intense. Both meet in the realm of touch. Waters feels into a person through touch and movement, the kinesthetic sense of knowing. They connect from the depths in a wordless, urgent, guttural way. Metal connects through the senses in a slow and detailed way that creates a cosmic connection.

Both are looking for connection, it's just that the connection is very different. Water is less about the senses and more about intensity, excitement, and moving things along. Metal is more about patient, detailed touch and intricate sensations that transport the lovers to another plane of existence together. If both Metal and Water can allow the intensity of Water to mingle with Metal's sacred touch, they can bridge the energetic gap.

Water/Wood: Dynamic Duo

At Wood's roots, Water quietly pools. *Water feeds Wood.* Wood can sometimes be very sensitive to the outside world and even be anxious. When Wood is in this state, Water is the best friend to have. Water patiently watches Wood participating in many activities and silently conveys the message, "I've got your back." For Wood, this non-verbal message is very comforting. In turn Wood loves being protected.

They love that level of support, and Water is usually quite happy to fill that need.

Wood is a fantastic audience for Water's silliness. There's no limit to how silly Water can be with Wood. With Wood, Water can take it to the extreme. Together they love to laugh. Wood sets the stage for Water's antics and the fun begins. Wood supports Water in many areas of life. Many successful Waters have had a Wood person backing them, guiding them, pushing them in new directions, and focusing them on the tasks at hand. *Wood delivers Water.*

Sometimes the "helpfulness" of Wood can be too much, however. Water can feel that Wood becomes too demanding, bossy, and overbearing, trying to force Water in a direction they may not want to go in. Another challenge in this Elemental match is that sometimes when Wood is feeling safe, they may realize they're looking for a partner who can keep up with them mentally and verbally. Water doesn't have the same level of wit. Even if Water is as smart as Wood, they might not be verbally as quick at humorous banter. Then Wood can start to feel lonely or bored intellectually. They need to engage. They also want to be challenged. Both Wood and Water need to compromise to work this out. Water has to be willing to step up to the verbal challenge and engage thoroughly in discussions. In addition Wood has to find outlets for their wit outside the relationship because it is unfair to ask any other Element to interact at the speed that Wood can.

The exception is a Water who has Wood as the second Element. The Water/Wood Elemental type is the most powerful of all the Elemental types, and the best comedian. They combine speed, quick-wit, and hilarious slapstick comedy that challenges Wood to keep up and laugh, which is a win-win in the Wood book of love.

In the bedroom, Wood and Water are a flurry of activity. Wood's strength and Water's power make for an unpredictable, dynamic duo. But as active as they can be in bed, they can find a quiet space together too. They share a desire to be peaceful and soft after sex, snuggling and being quiet. It's a great match sexually.

Controlling Relationships: Hang on for the Ride
Wood/Earth—Stick in the Mud

Wood and Earth make a great team because they share all the responsibilities in their relationship. In this sense we mean, ahem, Wood takes on the responsibility of delegating all the tasks and Earth delivers on completing those tasks. Sounds equal, right? Well it can work for many couples even though Wood and Earth are polar opposites. Wood is fast, Earth is slow. Wood is witty, Earth is thoughtful. Wood is strategic, Earth is analytical. Wood holds the big vision, Earth dots the i's and crosses the t's.

When the relationship works, they are solid together. But making it work requires a lot of sacrifices for both parties. It really is an exercise in patience for each (which is not Wood's strong point). Earth has to allow Wood to do whatever it wants to do, which often means sacrificing their own career aspirations. Wood is in charge, and they change constantly. Earth can take direction but doesn't like fast changes. They like slow transitions, so Wood usually takes Earth on a wild ride.

Earths love to support their partner. They enjoy helping their lover make big dreams come true. But they often prefer to take the back seat or a secondary role in these power dynamics. When Wood comes into an Earth's life, Earth is happy to do a lot of the nitty-gritty work for their partner while Wood climbs the ladder. Earths are doers and big givers, but not in the grand visionary sense that most Woods are. It's detail work Earth really excels at.

Even when Wood has serious wanderlust, they feel the need to put roots down for the Earth partner's sake. Since Earth wants security, Wood has to be tied down to responsibility and to providing for the home and family instead of pursuing every new project and idea striking their fancy. Then the relationship becomes less fun for Wood, especially after the kids come along. Wood can feel bogged down by sense of duty.

Obviously, the relationship exacts huge sacrifices from both, and if they make the necessary compromises they are often not living their true destiny. Such is the quandary of every Controlling Relationship—how to be true to yourself yet maintain a spicy relationship with two very opposite energies.

On the flip side, if Earth has a potential career that can take off, their Wood partner might be the one who actually manages it. Wood makes great managers, for business owners, celebrities, and artists. Wood can see the big picture and get huge projects to become reality very quickly.

In bed, the Wood/Earth dynamic is very connected and engaged. Earth will give of themselves knowing exactly what Wood wants. Earth is so available and wants to merge deeply with Wood. However, merging is different than engaging. Engaging is much more active than emotional. Both Wood and Earth are very focused on each other, a way in which they connect really well. Wood might end up taking more often than giving, which can upset the balance.

The different speeds at which Wood and Earth operate on will be very apparent. The Earth way of consciously sharing is slow, steady, and tuned in. For Wood sharing has a more vigorous pace, and the speed is variable—at different times. They like to mix it up with varied goals to please their lover. They never know what they want until they roll over.

Wood energy controls Earth. So when Earth takes a turn to give, and they give in their slow, luscious way, Wood may lose their mojo or interest. In order to return the balance and spark, Earth needs to engage more actively, learning how to give and receive at the same time with a faster pace and unpredictable rhythm. Wood has to find the challenge of satisfying Earth at a slower pace, perhaps focusing on a deeper sense of merging with the other person instead of physical activities alone.

Fire/Metal: White Hot Lovers

Fire is incredibly attracted to Metal because they see a secret mystery of love hidden inside Metal. They're not fooled by the quiet exterior. Fire will go to great lengths to find out what that secret is. They *need* to unravel they mystery. But the language of connection for Fire and Metal is very different. For Fire, it's heart-centered and emotional, requiring lots of words and talking for long stretches of time. For Metal lovers, it's all in their eyes. They don't require a lot of words. The eye contact can be very romantic and smoldering, which Fire may crave.

Metal may want a Fire partner because they like hanging back and letting that person run their life. It's very easy to play second fiddle when you're with Fire. They have so much exuberance for life, and they're fun to have around. Metal may actually enjoy social engagements but don't want to have to initiate them. How handy for them that their Fire partner handles all of that!

One of the challenges in this Elemental match is Fire's exuberance and never-ending *joie de vivre*, which Metal can find extremely annoying. Additionally, if Fire isn't living a real or authentic in life, Metal, which is serious about romance, will be put off. They can see right through those Fiery masks. If Fire is hiding something, the relationship probably won't get off the ground, no matter how much Fire pursues Metal. It's just not an option for Metal to be with someone who isn't really showing up or present in the world in a truly authentic way.

Fire and Metal can meet in a wonderful way of connecting. They represent two different kinds of energetic connections (the heart versus the sacred), but they both value the connection above all else. And when they find it together, it can be wonderful and beautiful, despite their energetic differences.

Fire's happy and outgoing persona emotionally conflicts with Metal's quiet and reserved nature. Metal can get really shut down emotionally. In the beginning especially, the couple can experience a lot of bickering about how to do things. The lovers are so very different in how they approach life, yet they make a wonderfully romantic couple if they can grow and accept their emotional differences and challenges.

Earth/Water: Murky Water

Earth is very attracted to Water. They like Water's deep, mysterious, powerful energy. They share a kind of similarity, a strong wordless connection they have sexually. Earth can take over in bed and be large and in charge. Water may like having a powerful person guiding and pushing them. They like to meet Earth's strength with their Water power. Their sexual experiences together can be extremely intense and powerful for both.

Earth likes to feel like they're merging completely with their lovers. Earth likes that Water connects from a very deep place. Earth falls in love with Water's unpredictable spontaneity, but later on, when its impulsiveness disturbs the daily rhythm of their lives, Earth can become annoyed. Water is about changing direction of the flow on the spur of the moment without planning. They do what they're motivated to do in the moment! Earth lives in the mind; Water lives in the now. It can be fun and sometimes exciting but also a little unsettling. Water can get out of control, spilling out all over the place, unable to focus. Water can really benefit from an Earth partner who can control the Water, and clean them up a bit. Earth provides the banks for the rivers so the rivers can gather momentum and flow faster. With Earth behind them, Water can be much more effective in life. If Water is very ambitious, having a capable and supportive guide can be the ingredient for success. Earth can be that guide!

The challenge is that Water sometimes loses power when they are with Earth. Water in this case can really go underground and almost stagnate. The Earth energy can be so powerful that Water can barely get traction. In fact, Earth undermines Water's ability to flow in some case. This is because Earth often considers all options before making a decision of what to do in many areas of their life. From big decisions to little ones, Earth looks at every angle. They analyze possible outcomes, especially things that could go wrong if you take a certain path. Water simply feels intuitively which way to go and trusts implicitly that they will know what to do at any moment. They don't fear a particular outcome and certainly don't like to fear any future event. However, having Earth around can really inject doubt into their trusting way of life, their very being.

Imagine Water is about to do something they haven't done before, and Earth comments, "I wouldn't do that because what if..." The Water is now frozen. They don't know what to do! Water can't move at all if fear is taking over. This is not overstating their plight. Having their confidence eroded is a very big problem for Water. Earth thinks they are being helpful by applying their powerful analytic ability to help the Water, but alas, the more they help, the more they are completely flipping the "off" switch to Water's power.

Earth needs to feel very emotionally connected before making love. Waters don't like talking about emotions as much, and would much prefer to kiss and make up in bed. Earth tortures their Water partner all night talking about their problems until Earth feels there's some kind of resolution. By then you're both exhausted, and there's no lovemaking that night. This is true of Earth in any romantic relationship, but their style is especially difficult for Water lovers, who would rather not talk about their emotions at all.

Making this relationship work requires a lot of relearning on both sides. Water must learn how to talk about emotions. It's imperative. Earth needs to learn to trust and go with the flow, allowing Water to do the things they find intense and exciting. That's why they fell in love in the first place. They're exciting and unpredictable. Let them be so!

Metal/Wood: Woodchopper

Metal likes Wood because they take things seriously like they do, and they'll get stuff done. If Metal has something they want to do that seems grand, Wood will listen and take it seriously. And who else to champion something important to Metal but the strong and amazing Wood partner they love dearly?

Metal likes that their Wood partners want to be in charge of everything. They like to hang back and watch. Yet, the only type of person Wood will bow to is Metal. Some Woods feel relieved when they have someone in their life that they actually want to take orders from. Metal can very quietly and respectfully tell Wood what to do, and they listen. But most of the time if someone of a different Elemental type tries to order Wood around, Wood will be resistant, even if it's the same exact thing Wood wanted to do five minutes before. They don't like being told what to do! However, Metal can come along and very quietly give an order, and Wood has no problem listening to that softer energy. Wood can deeply respect the Metal partner.

That doesn't mean that Metal and Wood don't conflict sometimes. All Controlling relationships are likely to have bickering. But what causes bickering? Disagreement is a by-product of these types of relationships. Metal/Wood is no exception. If Wood pushes, Metal will balk, and a disagreement is likely to follow. Guess who's in danger here? Metal's got the sharp blade, after all.

Sexually speaking, the two elements are very different. Metal lovers are slow and into experiencing the sense of touch. It can be very romantic. Wood is fast, enjoys humor, and wants to have a lot of physical activity in lovemaking. The two lovers will have to find common ground, likely in a spiritual connection. Both elements can be very romantic, loving, and deeply spiritual in their relationships.

Water/Fire—Fire Extinguisher

Water is very attracted to Fire. Water loves intensity, and who's more exciting than Fire? They love to laugh, joke, and be very social. Everybody likes Fire, so it's no surprise that Water often actively pursues Fire romantically. Once together they share a love of meaning and wisdom. Fire pursues knowledge and maturity in their life. Water pursues innate inner wisdom and knowing. They meet through the love of deep concepts and can have a hot and steamy sex life. Fire is the most passionate Element. Water is the most intense Element. When in a love relationship together, they share a very dramatic love!

The challenges come from the way they connect or disconnect. They both value connection but the types are very different. One Water once said that all Fires are just "surface dwellers." Fire connects through the heart, not the depths of their soul. They look into your eyes with love and affection but then look away shyly. Uninhibited and unabashed, Water looks into your soul and reaches in to grab you.

It's all or nothing with Water. They come alive in bed, and it's almost always on their terms. If *they* don't have the energy for sex, it ain't happening. When they want to have it, they'll pursue you relentlessly until you agree to have a romantic interlude. Really, Waters are going a hundred miles an hour or not at all. This stop/go behavior includes their sexual habits.

Another challenge for the Fire/Water couple is the Water's tendency to not need to talk or vocalize with their partners often. Water might not say "I love you" as often as Fire, who is guaranteed to say it many times a day.

The other issue is that Fire likes to socialize often. Water spends a lot of time reenergizing, sleeping, or resting, especially in the evenings if they've worked hard during the day. For this reason, they might be a social mismatch as a couple. They have to constantly negotiate and renegotiate social events, dinner parties, and the like.

If Water retreats inside themselves for a long time to recharge, Fire is left alone. Fires don't like to be solitary. They have to learn to be self-sufficient in that type of relationship. But when it's right, a Water/Fire match is a hot, sexy, and unpredictable tempest.

To make it together, Water has to remember that they fell in love with Fire because they are the life of the party, not a party-pooper. Water has to allow Fire to be exuberant and fun.

Ten

Love Potion #10
(Because the First Nine Didn't Work)

....

"As a self-described idealistic, I never
consider myself as single. I like to say that
I'm in between romances at the moment."

Carl Henegan

....

Have you been trying to make Mr. or Ms. Wrong into Mr.
or Ms. Right, over and over again? Do you idealize your lovers with traits you *want* them to possess, only to find out

months into the relationship that those attributes don't really exist in them? Have you had a bad break up recently or even years ago that still affects you? If you're "in between" romances, this is the chapter for you right here, right now. Don't go to bed until you finish this chapter. Really!

Evolution Revolution

Each Element has a growth cycle that matches your life. In Chinese Medicine, the actual acu-point names tell stories about how each Elemental type grows and evolves from birth to death.

These points make a road map that can be used as guidelines for us to follow. Sometimes we follow our path linearly. Other times we circle back to the beginning and start over. There is no right or wrong; there are no mistakes.

The evolution of the Elements is the path you get to pick—your potential. Are you ready for an evolution? And are you ready for *your* evolution?

In-Betweeners

Finding love is only one part of your journey. According to Chinese Medicine, there are nine palaces (goals) to pursue in life, including career, children, health, and of course relationships, among others. Whether within ourselves or in a relationship, we all have an innate drive to pursue love.

The questions to ask yourself are: Where are you right now in your life? Are you happy with your life? Do you really want a serious relationship at this point? Maybe you've just left a long-term relationship and need to have some fun. Or maybe you're really ready to settle down with a partner.

These questions are not ordinary or run-of-the-mill; they go deep to our core. They are about life's journey and about the relationships we have during our time on this planet.

If you look from this point forward into your future, what pathway do you want your life to take? How would you want to spend it over the next five, ten, or even twenty years? Elementally speaking, your life is constantly changing, growing, shifting, and moving you along, maybe without you being aware of it. Many of your needs and desires in love and life will change as you mature. By understanding yourself and what you really want in love, you can be much more effective in finding the right partner.

To best use this chapter, find your Element and read about your options and combinations. A first step in finding your love match is to ask yourself what kind of love you *really* want. Here's your chance to dream out loud.

Omphaloskepsis of Love (Look It Up)

Have you ever met someone you sort of like, but as you date, it's clear that this person isn't the love of your life? Maybe you continue to date because nothing else is going on and it's comfortable. Then you start to rationalize the relationship's ongoing status saying things like: "Well, he's a really nice person," "I'm having a nice time with her," or "I'm lucky someone actually likes me." The excuses people invent to stay in half-fulfilling relationships are endless. The relationship continues until you stop letting anyone else appear on your romantic radar because you're investing so much in this mediocre, lukewarm, "nice" relationship. Now fast forward: you've moved in together or you're getting married—wait for it… it's coming… and soon enough you feel stuck, bored out of your mind, and totally unfulfilled.

If this scenario represents a familiar and repeated pattern for you, it's time to stop and evaluate the qualities you are attracting in love. Maybe at some point you threw common sense out the window and adopted a flippant "what-the-heck" attitude in hopes that the lover you settled for would magically transform into that perfect person you want. Are you still waiting? Nothing yet, huh? What now?

Or another scenario could be that you had a bad breakup (insert how long ago here). Perhaps you're shut down emotionally and the walls are up. You are locked high in your tower, and nobody's getting past the moat. Not even a giant ogre could save you! It won't happen this time because you're stuck. You could end up in voluntary (or involuntary) celibacy for years or in an endless series of one-night stands. You're not going to break out of your pattern with more of the same. If you want to make some changes in your perspective and in your prospects… read on, princesses and princes.

That being said, this is not a Hollywood movie or children's fairytale. Nor is it a scientific experiment. This is your life, your heart, and your journey. No one will know it better than your own self.

If you're looking for love, the first thing you have to do (mentioned earlier in this book) is to really be honest with yourself. That's the first step, and these are all baby steps. So baby, be honest right now. Breathe in deep and take a long look at yourself. What are all the beautiful, wonderful, fantastic parts that make you who you are? Look at them. Ponder them. Now exhale. Wow, you can hold your breath a long time! Breathe in again. Now you won't have to look as hard. Glance thoughtfully (but quickly) on the not-so-pretty (dare we say ugly?) traits that may be making you unhappy. Exhale. Congratulations, you're moving forward. If you're the type who likes to write stuff down, this would be a good place to start.

Matchmaker, Matchmaker...

Let's talk about how to pick the right person who's compatible energetically with you at this time in your life. The choice has much more to do with energetics than we realize. Remember, energy rules this planet. You have all Five Elements within you. You could theoretically make any relationship work for you at any time in your life. Not to get ahead of ourselves, but chapter eleven is about long-term relationships and how to succeed no matter what combination of Elements brought love into your life.

For now, if you are in between romances and looking for love, it's time to imagine your ideal romantic encounter. This chapter is more about understanding which Element would better fit into your life at this time. It is about you taking control of your life in a positive and healthy way. If you're still not clear what Element you are, consider your top two. This chapter will help you to clarify them and gain more insight into each Element.

Wood—Branching Out

Wood is on a path of growth that evolves from a sprout to sapling to a full-grown tree. The trip may entail a lot of challenges that take place over a lifetime. You may always be in this middle sapling phase, engaging the world. You might always be on the lookout for injustices and wrongs to right. You fight the good fight, win, receive the reward, and repeat with the next good cause. Or, you may find yourself returning to a sprout-like life due perhaps to a trauma or the occasional illness. You know you've arrived at your final tree stage when the external battles are complete and you are working at finding peace in yourself. This phase can in more rare cases be achieved at a young age. The path need not be linear, and this cycle can repeat many times over in a lifetime.

Twist and Sprout—Stage One

Are you at a point in your life when you're feeling timid and small, not wanting to step out and risk anything? This is not a bad thing—it's just a stage. Child-like, you might have some anxiety in front of other people. Perhaps you just want to run away. Or you may even fear for your safety or your general survival. Even as an adult you could return to the sprout stage as a result of difficulties or trauma. It could be short- or long-term.

As a sprout, you have to find a way to grow despite your obstacles, such as a bad relationship, an unsatisfying job, violence, and/or financial insecurity. If this is where you find yourself, you'd benefit from a *nourishing* relationship. Water could be a complementary romantic match at this time in your evolution. You need someone who can truly water your roots. So how could this Water romance really help you?

Water is going to make you feel very peaceful and safe. They have a lot of power, and they don't have the need to talk constantly. Although they are quiet, Water loves to make you laugh. They are the comedians of life, and Wood loves laughter. Water also cares about safety, and they're very observant about the world around them. No other Element has your back as well as Water. Because you are in a vulnerable state, having a partner who's got your back and is really there for you is such a relief for a Wood who may feel anxious in this sprout-like stage. Wood floats on Water; it holds the weight of the world for you.

This is a stage where Wood doesn't want to be really *big* in life. Water is totally comfortable with Wood being quieter. Woods have a very quiet side; the inside is all about peace, and Water enhances that peace. Being with Water can really help you heal. Their presence is like a silent encouragement for you to step out in the world and feel safe. Some Woods go their whole lives without ever really being big, and that's okay.

Wood in the sprout stage will also love Water's adventurous spirit. They can transform a period of insecurity into a carefree spree of great fun without bearing responsibility for your world. Together you can make plans to do exciting things. Water has a goal of being intense, whether it's sitting on the couch or bungee jumping. They seek out intensity. So they might be great partners to train for a difficult obstacle course race. Or they might love to climb very tall mountains with you. Together you both win! Wood gets to achieve the goals (getting to the mountain, climbing up the mountain, climbing down the mountain). Water gets to have the experience of being at the top.

Little Big Shot—Stage Two

As Wood entering in your second stage of life, you engage the world. Typically you become more confident and bold, like a sapling breaking through hard winter ground and growing speedily toward the sky. You battle in the world for good and amazing purposes. Maybe you're an athlete battling for a gold medal or just a weekend warrior. Or you might be a do-gooder, fighting for the rights of others or a business person, grasping for the top position in the market.

This phase is really about leadership and being willing to be big in your life. You can take on greater responsibility and be a leader in business or your community. Your leadership can be as simple as getting your neighbors to talk to each

other and steering your community to more friendly interactions, like organizing a block party. Wood doesn't have to
be a CEO. You can be a leader among all your good friends,
someone that everyone looks up to.

At this point in your life, you are ready to take on the
world, and you feel capable and self-reliant so you don't feel
a need for help to grow your roots. You might want to have
some help tackling the world. Who's the best helper, worker,
and doer? Is there an Earth in the house?

Wood has the vision, Earth does the details. It's a winning
combination. Earth goes along for the ride and lets Wood do
whatever it needs to do to achieve their current goals. Wood
calls the shots. Earth supports Wood in being big and out
in the world, yet the two Elements find a balance of equality and respect. Wood needs to be powerful in order to take
on a strong Earth personality without being snapped like a
twig. Wood saplings are focused and upwardly mobile, literally. They have the self-direction and motivation the strength
to engage Earth's solidness and channel it into projects (lots
and lots of projects). They figuratively grow roots within the
Earth, creating a life and a family together while engaging and
changing the world.

As the Worm Turns—Stage Three

Wood's stage-two engagement with the world can span many
years. But the real growth mostly happens later in life when
they're done fighting the good fight. They come to realize that the real battle is internal within themselves. It's a

spiritual battle. They begin to see that material goods aren't as valuable as they thought. They'll still help people, but they're much more selective about the projects they pick because the accolades and rewards for their good deeds don't bring fulfillment as they once did. Finally they begin to look inside. And that inward road will last the rest of their lives.

If you are Wood, your spiritual journey requires digging up the past and looking at yourself and how well you behaved or not. An important acu-point on the Wood energetic meridian is called "Wormwood." Representing this stage of the life journey, wormwood is like maggots turning over and over in the garbage to clean out the debris. Okay, that sounds a little gross, but the important thing here is the process of inner growth and reflection Wood requires for the completion of its third stage.

The questions Wood may ask introspectively at the beginning of this stage might be: "Did I hurt anyone in the past while I fought for the greater good? How do I feel about those casualties? Were they fair decisions? Was I being selfish? Could I have done it differently? Could I have done it better?"

If you feel yourself engaging the outside world less and are more engaging yourself, your morals, your purpose in life … if you're on your spiritual journey inside yourself, then you may want to share this time with a Fire partner. This person would likely be more mature, someone who has learned how to be authentic in themselves and who is not afraid to lose love. A Fire who can really meet you on your level has to have also gone through a lot of internal growth in themselves. For Fire, this means they have to truly love themselves.

This combination of Wood and Fire is very dynamic. Together Fire and Wood can laugh all day long. Wood has worked so hard for so long. Life is about having some fun finally. Who better to have some fun with than Fire!

More importantly, the depth of acceptance and unconditional love that Fire offers is something Wood is going to need during their period of introspection and reassessment. What if you think you could have done things better and the meaning of your life is in question? Wood has difficulty processing their darker shadow sides, normally preferring to gloss over the bad and focus on only the good. Fire will love you even if you think you've screwed up. Fire engages the dark side (though not quite like Darth Vader's), and often in their quest to love themselves, Fire must look at all their own imperfections. But as Woods progress through this stage, they no longer need to rise to the top at any cost. They become able to integrate the good and bad and end up with a quieter greatness that doesn't require outer deeds as proof. Instead, inner peace becomes the end goal.

Fire—Striking a Match

The Fire growth path is about exploding into life, full of love and joy. You want to share your light with the world, but you discover (often very early on) that there are mean people in the world. The journey for Fire is to experience this meanness, allow the hurt, and evolve to a new place where you are un-affected by it.

Firestarter—Stage One

The first stage of the Fire's life is to learn how to negotiate the sometimes-harsh world. You might find that you just can't be yourself unless you feel safe with the people in your life. This might mean you try to fit in, making you vulnerable to peer pressure in school, work, romance, or your family. When people are mean, you might even think that you're bad or something's wrong with you, so you might make your world small to ensure a sense of safety. This means that social life can be limited.

When you are feeling very unsafe, you fear people and have difficulty being out in the world. What makes you feel safe is feeling like you fit in. You want so badly to look good, you are susceptible to doing or saying anything you think will gain acceptance. At this time in your life, an Earth romance may feel the safest for you. Earth is so caring and wants you to be comfortable. They'll listen to your fears and help you work through them. Earths are also socially active, so it's easier for a Fire to go out in public with an Earth lover.

Earth is likely to listen to you and validate your experience. They can help you process the mean things that have happened to you in the past. They don't mind talking for hours and hours about your problems. And when you help them by listening to theirs, they are very appreciative and grateful, which makes you feel special. In the end, even though Fire usually nourishes Earth, the relationship is symbiotic. Fire gives to Earth, which makes the Fire feel bigger and more mature. Being a good companion, Earth builds Fire up, showing them how great they are.

Fanning the Flames—Stage Two

As you begin to feel more comfortable with yourself and life, you may want to throw yourself into your work, gathering as much knowledge about things as you can. You can use that knowledge as a buffer against the world. If you know a lot, people will treat you with respect. So you can get really accomplished in work and achieve a higher social status. People enjoy your company and like to have you around all the time. Another endearing feature is that you're great at throwing parties. Although the compliments feel really good, you're still cautious about people's intentions, which means you're not ready to trust being yourself in their company.

Having a Fire/Fire romance is good at this time in your life. Being with another Fire relieves your social anxiety. The knowledge that you have each worked so hard in acquiring helps you both succeed socially. You can strive together to achieve social acceptance in the upper echelon. You'll both accept each other's preoccupations with the social hierarchies of your respective circles, and you can be comfortable with each other's successes. Still, having knowledge doesn't mean you are comfortable being truly authentic. Two masks work really well in the social world but can come off at night, where you can fan each other's flames of passion. You can both share your exuberance for life—and sex!

Another great combination at this stage is Fire/Metal. Metal's devout love and romantic flare can really boost Fire's need for unconditional love. When Metal makes a commitment to Fire, Fire rests assured that they are completely safe in love. They can move on to greater spheres in the social and work realms, acquiring knowledge, and making connections.

Sacred Fires—Stage Three

As Fire continues to mature, you begin to learn how to not take things so personally. The maturity of Fire is about going backwards, back to infancy when you took nothing personally and just radiated joy naturally.

You begin to drop the masks you created in the social world and let your true self show. You fall in love with *this* true self. In this stage of your Fiery journey, living authentically is your goal. You develop that authenticity by learning to take unkind acts with equanimity. You just don't care about others' approval as you once did. This independence frees you to be more yourself. This is your ultimate goal as Fire: the best protection is no protection.

Think of it like being a tai chi master. When a tai chi master is attacked, they simply stand aside as a punch or kick is thrown. The attacker ends up falling on their face, and the master walks away unscathed. In other words, if someone is trying to be mean to you, you can't get hurt unless you take the hit. If you sidestep it emotionally, you just realize that the attacker has problems, and it's not you.

If you travel backwards on the Fire energetic meridian associated with protecting the Heart, you return to the first point, Heavenly Pond, which connects you to the source from which you came. The time has come to drop all the protection you've worked so hard on building. *It's time to no longer care what other people think.*

When Fire can be completely authentic, they may enjoy a Wood partner, especially one in a later, reflective Wormwood stage. But before this time, a Fire/Wood relationship can be very challenging because Wood really demands authenticity. They won't stand for imposters. In this last stage Fire has less of a need for social stimulation and acceptance and more the need of the inner joy that comes from being in love.

Wood is Fire's best motivator. Through encouragement, it stokes the Fires, helping them feel less afraid to truly be themselves. Wood allows Fire to burn brightly. They feel safe because Wood is big and doesn't fear or shy away from interaction with the world. In this way Wood nourishes Fire, giving them the confidence to shine authentically, not just in bed, but in the world.

Earth—Plowing the Fields

The growth path for Earth starts in early childhood when their nourishment and love is derived from their mothers. In their second stage, fully fed and loved, Earth moves out into the big world, curious with innocent, wide eyes. But Earth is astonished to see so many problems in the world and may feel compelled to help those in need. When very few people return the favors, Earth can become disappointed, resentful, and even closed off to the help offered them. In the final stage, Earth stops wanting help from others and receives what comes to them miraculously in life, like a field receiving rain for nourishment freely and without effort. This they turn around and give without wanting anything in return.

Little Earthquakes—Stage One

The first Earth stage begins as a baby, when you receive the love and nurturing of your parents. Most babies experience this, but for Earth it's more poignant and important than it is for others. Even in adulthood, the quality of parental love (good or bad) is what they remember most from childhood. Many Earth children even resist growing old and wish they could be children forever. The desire for parental nurturing may last well into adulthood, which is normal for Earth. Their entire lives will be about giving and receiving, and no one will ever give to them as selflessly as their parents (assuming they had giving ones). Truth be told, Earth never stops wanting nourishment, and life's question for them is, where can it be found after leaving home?

If you are Earth, long after your actual mother has stopped nurturing you, you may still experience an intense need for similar warmth and nurturing. Or worse, maybe you didn't get much nurturing at home growing up, and now you feel as if there is a deficit, as if your Earth is parched and dry from a long drought. If you recognize this fact about yourself, you may try to hide it from others, even refusing to receive anything, becoming fiercely, stubbornly independent. And without realizing these unconscious desires for nurturing, you might be asking your partner to fill that void.

If you're at a place in your life where you really want nourishment and comfort (like wanting to go home and crawl into mother's lap), it's completely normal and okay. Accept this fact in yourself, which is partly giving yourself the love a mother might bestow. Then through your acceptance, allow yourself to receive in your next relationship. In this case, you might seek out a Fire partner. They will shower you with love and warmth and make life feel at ease. If you have problems, they will talk them over with you. They love talking, and you may as if you need to talk and talk. Earth gets to soak up all that heat from Fire's warming glow.

Life Support—Stage Two

Eventually, this child wants to go out into the big world and experience life. Because the Earth gift to the world is problem-solving. Earth is often aware of problems around them. The big world seems to have lots of troublesome problems and worrisome scenarios. It's almost impossible to not be overwhelmed with them when you first look out into the world as you contemplate leaving your warm, safe home. When embarking on your journey through life, leaving you, you may feel compelled to become everyone's mother and take care of them. You may find yourself giving and giving and giving yet again.

If you're at a place in your life when you're focused on life's problems—either your own or in your community and the world—you might want to find a partner who is equally as giving. In other words, will your partner be able to support you at the end of the day? An Earth romantic partner might be perfect in this phase because you're giving so much and may get quite depleted if your partner requires a lot of your attention and gifts at the end of the day. The world can be tiring, and Earths sometimes complain that all they want is a partner who can help and support them. They may feel unappreciated and can even become quite frustrated because no one empathizes with them enough to offer them help. Their efforts are so exhausting and thankless. Having another Earth by your side—someone who really understands and empathizes—giving you comfort and nurturing is profoundly welcome. What a relief!

Journey to the Center of the Earth— Stage Three

The third path for Earth is realizing you can have everything you need from life, like a tree self-supported in the rain and sunshine. The last point on the Earth meridian, called "Great Fruition" or "Embracing Life" helps you feel the unconditional nourishment of life, as if you are still in the womb. It's basically the point of "ask and you shall receive." They become connected to that mysterious source of energy, what the Chinese refer to as "Source" or the divine, which provides them with unlimited resources to give. It's as if they soak up all their nourishment through the cosmos. The fact that they give and give no longer feels taxing, and they no longer feel resentful when people do not reciprocate. They can move energy and transform things to create and give the best they have to offer to every person they meet.

If you've arrived at a stage in your life when you no longer feel you need things from others, you will enjoy a love relationship with Metal because they can receive all that you give without making you feel drained. They will serve you with undying loyalty, completing many tasks you require. They will immensely appreciate all the support you give them and all the social networking you will do on their behalf. But they won't ask for more than you can give. As you let go concern with the day-to-day worries of life, you can embrace your spiritual center. And who better to do that with than Metal, who is in touch with the deeper sacred mysteries of life.

Metal—Magnets of Love

The journey of Metal's growth in life moves from wanting to be close to home and family to letting go and being the cool or respected person in society to ultimately flying free from social attachments.

Panning for Gold—Stage One

The first stage for Metal is attachment. As a child, Metal feels very connected to home and family and finds staying close to home natural and easy, so long as that family is safe and nourishing. If your parents weren't safe to attach to, you might feel attached to friends, siblings, or grandparents…anyone who doesn't mind you clinging to them. The death of any of these nurturing people can be derailing and devastating, perhaps throwing you off for years at a time.

In some cases, such people might struggle to "launch" themselves in life. Letting go of your safe home life can be hard. Having a relationship with Earth can be the transition needed during your attachment phase of life. Earths make great family surrogates, especially if your family wasn't very caring or loving. They will create a great home for you and be very devoted to you. They'll also help you move slowly out into the world by gently bringing you out to socialize with others.

Chillaxing—Stage Two

Eventually you leave the comfort of your childhood home and family and launch into the wider world, whether you want to jump or not. Yet you adapt, learning how to be really different (because you are) and yet fit in through appearing really cool or respectable (because you can). At first, you might feel awkward and estranged as a new member of a peer group. Perhaps you are detecting negative feedback and worry that your peers are critical or unkind. Instead of being cool, you might feel like an outcast. But eventually you will find a niche and be the coolest person in your group. You might also feel very attached to the new friends and lovers who come into your life.

When you move out into the world, your best companion might be Water. They are very exciting and like to do lots of things. Water will get you to be adventurous, and you both will laugh like crazy together. Water's also really good at just hanging out, which of course is great for your romance. The best part is you can be weird with Water, which is a huge relief. Metal balks at being put in a social box, but with Water, you can float downstream in life instead of feeling compelled to be mainstream.

Pedal to the Metal—Stage Three

In the third stage, you find a way to be completely free in your life. You lovingly connect with important friends and lovers without needing to cling to them. You also respect yourself and don't look outside for people to validate and appreciate you. You are connected in the moment but still detached, letting go with grace those who move out of your life. You're free-flying and loving life.

The point on the Metal meridian that symbolizes this freedom is called the "Great Abyss." It's like falling into a void where nothing exists except a chasm. Instead of feeling terror at such a prospect, you feel relief, leaving all the cares and woes of life behind while you fly through time and space.

If you're in a stage in your life when you're riding freely on your magic carpet ride, who better to join you than another Metal? It's a wild wonderful ride, and another Metal can be laid back with you. Of course, that person has to be in a similar place in life, allowing things to come and go out of their life, not attaching in any way. This means that you can't demand a lifetime commitment from your partner. It's all about loving life in the moment, not forcing someone to be stagnant and predict the future. The good news is that when two Metals get together and are very happy, it's likely to last a lifetime. When it's right, Metals are often in it for the long run.

Water—Oceans in Motion

In the way that the Ocean symbolizes all the states of water simultaneously (rapid movement on top, relentless waves lapping the shores, and powerful, slow currents deep down below), Water's journey through life isn't really a linear progression of growth. Water constantly alternates between stillness and motion, which means that their paths are often much more varied and unpredictable.

If we look at a progression from childhood through life, you could look at the Water meridian that starts with the acupuncture point called "Bubbling Spring" at the bottom of your feet. Waters emerge from the womb giggling and flowing easy but not forcefully (yet). Since this bubbling Water isn't moving fast, it will begin to dry up in the hot sun as it starts to trickle forward, as symbolized by the next point, "Blazing Valley." It has to pool and gather rainwater before it has the power to move forward again. It settles into a "Great Ravine," the third point on the meridian, to refill and gather power. Then it will start moving again. This pattern of moving forward and stagnating to gather power continues to alternate throughout life. You feel very tentative and reluctant to move at first. Then you might build up the ambition to flow. And finally you might come to rest in order to gather more power. Occasionally Water freezes during stressful and scary times and needs to thaw before it can flow again.

Ice, Ice Baby—Stage One

Either as a child or later in life, many Waters experience times of heightened anxiety or fear. Being afraid of a particular outcome, desperately trying to avoid it from happening, means that you must stand completely still and not move, figuratively and literally. If you don't move, the bad thing won't happen. Sometimes your entire life can be put on hold as you remain in fear's grip.

If you are going through a time in your life when you're feeling very fearful, like a frozen pond, you might want to be with Fire, who will help you melt the ice. They have no problem facing the scariest possibilities. They'll help you realize that you are equipped with everything you need to overcome the potential hardships. Fires always look at the bright side of everything. They will help you feel more optimistic about the hazards you must confront, the risks you will take, and the path ahead. They reassure you that what you need right now is to move forward and start flowing again.

Up the River with a Paddle—Stage Two

If you're feeling at ease and able to boldly embrace the world, like flowing water, you move out according to whatever speed is comfortable to you. This might be a very slow trickle, but that's what you're comfortable with at the moment. However, you might have bigger aspirations. Maybe you want to flow like a raging river, leading you to a specific adventure.

If you feel ambitious in this stage, you might want a Wood by your side. One of the important Water points on the body is called "Ambition Room." Ambition won't get you anywhere without action, so you need Wood to help you plan, focus, and execute your ideas. Romantically, you will both feel very activated and love to do many things together. Water and Wood can have a shared sense of humor. Water cannot be with someone who doesn't laugh and who refuses to be silly. This stage of your life will be active and exciting. Wood will keep you moving and together you two will have amazing and fulfilling experiences.

Slow Mo'—Stage Three

If you're feeling tired and need to be less active, and more peaceful, you're more like a still pond. What's the hurry? Where do you really need to go?

At this point, you might want a relationship with a Metal whose calmness can fuel the power you're generating through stillness. Metal nourishes Water, so Water gathers power from Metal. Metal also allow you to really rest and rejuvenate when you're both hanging out. So you spend more time than you'd normally do chilling. Relaxation helps you regain and collect your energy (as opposed to Wood, which will draw upon your energy simply by getting you to do more activities.)

Water and Metal also can share a love of the weirder side of humor that is powerful and bonding.

Twin Rivers—Stage Four (Because Three's Not Enough)

But let's just say you're feeling like alternating your adventures with your still times. One day you're a river flowing, the next day you're a still pond. Another compatible romantic combination at this time in your life is Water/Water.

Two Waters have a blast all the time, whether they're climbing a mountain or sitting on a couch watching TV or playing video games. They have the same quirky sense of humor, the same desire to be adventurous, and the same propensity for being homebodies the rest of the time to relax. Two Waters together experience a welcome relief when they can lounge romantically without the pressure of having to keep busy and active all the time.

Who's on Second?

These romantic pairings are just the beginning of the possibilities you could discover on your love journey. The second of your Five Elements often plays a very important part of your Elemental Energetic makeup.

Before we talk about how second Elements affect a relationship, we first need to explain how your second Element enhances your first Element. Here is a short summary of what a second Element looks like in each person.

Wood Second	Wood adds strength and the ability to accomplish goals. If you're Earth/Wood, this means you are the project person with the details and doingness of Earth and the vision of Wood. That's powerful. If you're Fire/Wood, that means you're much stronger in the social sphere. Water/Wood is the most powerful person on the planet (the power of Water backed by the strength of Wood). They are unafraid to speak boldly and loudly. Metal/Wood is more sure and strong about enforcing the rules in life (the best combo for a judge).
Fire Second	Fire adds charm and optimism. If you're Earth/Fire, you have incredible sociability. Wood/Fire are the master spin doctors, making anything sound good. Metal/Fire are quiet but charming and alluring. Water/Fire are bubbly and humorous.
Earth Second	Earth adds more thoughtfulness and talkativeness. Fire/Earth can be excellent leaders, warm and considerate. Wood/Earth have the vision but take their time completing tasks thoughtfully. Metal/Earth are quiet but very talkative one-on-one. Water/Earth are the still pond types but can be very chatty.

Metal Second	Metal adds reverence and softness. Wood/Metal are firm with a sharp, sarcastic wit. Fire/Metal are quiet, connecting through bright, warm eyes. Earth/Metal are incredibly organized and doing, with a little less need to socialize than other Earth types. Water/Metal are the quietest socially of all the Elemental types, often avoiding unnecessary social events.
Water Second	Water adds ambition and drive. Wood/Water is incredibly serious and driven to accomplish goals. Fire/Water often pursue knowledge and status with gusto. Earth/Water have a strong drive and ambition, which can be applied to community building. Metal/Water are the most energized Metal types, moving quickly and very motivated to do many different things.

Two Scoops Are Better than One!

When you consider making a romantic match, knowing the first and second Elements of both people provides a whole new layer of depth to understanding the relationship.

We have discovered after many years of evaluating couples that the number one reason why people get together and stay together is due to the influence of the second Element. When your second Element matches the first Element of your lover, then you may have a great match. For example, if you're Earth/Water and you get together with a Wood/Earth lover, you have enough variety (the first Element is different) to make things interesting, but you also have enough sameness (this Wood can speak the Earth language with you) to make it work. Occasionally, we see couples who have the same second Element, which is also useful. We even know a couple that has the same first and second Elements. Imagine that! Having that much sameness feels like you've finally come home and the person you're with really *gets* you.

Surprisingly, few couples share the first Element, like Wood/Wood. Most people want some variety in their relationship, so for some, a Same/Same relationship may lack the mystery and adventure of romance. But when your first Element is the same as your partner's second Element, you get both the spiciness of variety with enough similarities that getting along is easy.

That said, it's not easy to determine a second Element in someone else. Suffice it to say that if you're very attracted to someone who is different from you, you probably share some commonalities in your second Elements. For most, the best formula is a blend of sameness and difference.

Eleven

Going the Distance

....

"Being deeply loved by someone gives you strength,
while loving someone deeply gives you courage."

Lao Tzu

....

You've loved him forever. You know she's *the one*. It used to be so easy, but it's just been so difficult lately. And now that the kids have grown and are leaving the nest, everything is called into question. Why stay?

These are the big challenges couples may ponder in a long-term relationship. Sometimes they have small children and are already questioning their future. But many have put up with a difficult energetic dynamic for ten, fifteen, even twenty plus years and are realizing it just seems too hard to stay together once the children are gone. Why bother? It hasn't been good for a long time. We stayed together for the children, or the pets, or to pay off the house. People in this position question everything, even themselves.

Love but Not In Love?

If you want to try to make it work, what does it take to resurrect your relationship? It makes sense to examine closely what you have (or had) together that's special. Don't give up! It may be salvageable. It may be worth it to both of you to reignite and reconnect. You might really love each other, but can you fall "in love" again?

The Five Elements can help you understand and accept your differences. You can recognize each other's gifts as well as your unhealthy, negative patterns. Once you see these negative patterns, you can undo them and start anew.

The Only Person You Can Change is Yourself...

This chapter may be a little hard to stomach. It's not always pretty when your relationship breaks down and negative energy dynamics continue to build up over time. Walls go up and feelings get hurt. People shut down. The reality is, you could be contributing in a way that's not good for the relationship. You might not like the person you've become. You don't want to be mean to your partner, but you can't help it.

How can you reverse this pattern? How can you get into a good place, forgive, and open your heart again?

Opening your eyes is the first step to opening your heart. Stage one of working with the Five Elements is acceptance: accepting yourself, your partner, and the people you surround yourself with (children, parents, friends, etc.). The truth is, if you don't work on your own challenges, it really doesn't matter how many times you start over with somebody new; you may find you have similar problems in future relationships.

If you learn to accept your partner's way of being, you can move forward on changing the things that hurt the relationship. What's the point of connecting with all the goodness inside of you if your partner remains unwilling to change or even look at what needs to be done? It takes two to tango. Both partners have to want and be willing to put in the work, not just one. If that's not the case, then you'll have to face the harsh reality that it's time to move on. Gulp!

Before you read on, it's important to go back and look again at your Element. Working on yourself is really the key to solving problems in your relationship. You have the power to change your part, though keep in mind that you can never force another person to change. How have you been blocking the happiness and fun your two could be having?

Next review your partner's Element. What kind of relationship do you have energetically? Are you the Same Element, a Parent or Child Element, or do you have a Control Cycle relationship? Review the dynamics of your Elemental combination.

Now, let's take a look at each Element and the challenges they present in any loving relationship. What are you going to have to accept (and stop trying to change) and what are you able to change? The following explains what it's like to be partnered with each Elemental Energetic type.

Accepting Wood: Going with the Grain

When you're partnered with Wood, you need a sense of humor. You need to help your Wood partner laugh all the time at the little nuances of life. If you're not laughing in your relationship, that could be a key that opens your heart. At some point in the relationship, there must have been a lot of laughter. Where did it go? At some point the humor stopped. Maybe it even turned ugly. Wood is serious out in the world; more likely than not, they don't want to be serious with their intimate partners. They see the humor and irony in everything.

When you're in a relationship with Wood, you need to get used to being ordered around. Sorry, that's how they are. On a normal day, it can be gentle, but as the stress rises, so will their level of control. Planning a big vacation, remodeling the house, overcoming difficulties with the children ... Wood will step up and take control.

It's as if Woods feel safer when they know where you are and what you're going to be doing. If you're going to walk the dog, your Wood partner will tell you where to go as a matter of fact, not aggressively. They don't really care if you go that way. They're just compelled to say it. You may ask yourself, "What does it matter to them which way I go?" Well, it's just their nature. It's not personal. It may seem like an attack, but they're not angry or mad. They're just trying to get it done. They can't help it; it's who they are. They are the generals, and they're made to give orders.

Your relationship could suffer greatly if you become angry or get sick of this gift of Wood as master delegators. You can't expect them to do otherwise. You need to learn the skills of letting Wood say what they want, take it with a grain of salt, and do what you need to do. They actually want you to be equal to them. They don't want you to be crying about the tone of their voice being too harsh. They're trying to expedite the situation—make everything work as efficiently as possible. They want you to understand and roll with the situation. What just happened is now over and done. It's a surge of energy that moves forward like an arrow with direct force and then comes to a stop and rests.

This doesn't mean you have to be their verbal punching bag. They need to learn how to be respectful and not mean, condescending, or basically a jerk. They need to learn how to be respectful and not mean, condescending, or basically a jerk. (Continuously giving presents to make up for being a jerk or for feeling guilty isn't going to improve your relationship either.)

If you're partnered with Wood, you need to learn to listen. If they give you an order and you're not listening, they get very frustrated. They have a much bigger plan, and they were counting on your assignment to be fulfilled. You are a cog in the wheel, and the whole plan rests on something that seems quite minor from your vantage point. It might be as simple as dinner. They might ask you to pick up an ingredient. But if you're spacing out and subsequently forget, then the whole timing of the evening is going to be thrown off. Now someone has to go back to the store at an inconvenient time to fill in the gap. Nothing is more frustrating to Wood than inefficiency. They're even frustrated with themselves if they forget (which they do at times). Remember the laughter? When dinner's ruined, so what! Laugh and order out. Line's too long at the movies? So what, we'll go bowling. You need to change the flow, go with the flow, be part of the flow.

I'm Sorry I'm Always Right. You'll Get Used to It.

Somehow Woods know things that aren't necessarily logical. And they can't always explain to you why you should do something. After a while, though, you might notice that they're almost always right. They're usually gracious enough not to say "I told you so" many times a day, unless they can say it as a joke and know you'll take it well. They are actually very kind and never want to be hurtful.

When you're in public, they may also enjoy a little humor, saying something quite bold. This might embarrass some people. Imagine walking into a shop and your Wood partner announces to the staff and everyone else in the store:"Find something hot and sexy for *this* one!"

To understand your Wood partner, you must understand that their gift is to be assertive and engage people all the time. They can't help it. Woods engage in many ways, some big, some small. One example is creating challenges in a community in order to effect change and benefit many people. One Wood recently told us how he wanted to fix a community problem and promised to pay a large sum of money if the town could figure out how to improve the street parking. This created an uproar in his community, and embarrassed his wife greatly. He was sad that she didn't understand his intentions since he thought he was doing something for the greater good. He thought it was going to make a win-win situation for everyone, including himself, since the parking situation was near their house. Wood stirs things up to create change. Wood is the wind. When the wind blows, things change.

Some people like to be goal-free and meander around, looking at nature. Others like to sit quietly and watch. Wood can do either of those of course, for short periods of time, but they're more likely to create a challenge or game out of their experience. They are engaging with their own experience of something. If they're about to climb a mountain, they might time it, or figure out the most direct route, or come up with some other challenge for themselves or the people they're with. Be prepared to be pushed or challenged all the time. And the rewards can be great and fun, if you're up for it.

If you're very different, you might have to explain this to your Wood partner ... they just don't understand the concept of not having a goal to complete. Maybe you just want to climb the mountain to breathe the fresh air, look at the trees, be one with nature, and not make a challenge or competition out of it. You can let your Wood partner do it their way or you can teach them a new way of being in life, if they're open to that. But there's no sense being upset by their goal-orientated nature. They will seek out goals every day of their life, no exception.

Accepting Fire:
Mirror, Mirror, on the Wall

When you're partnered with Fire, you need to fall in love with them every day. If you remind them every day that they're good and that you think they look great, that will bring enormous ease in your relationship. They need a little reassurance ... how they look, whether they've said the right thing, if they're doing a good job. All you have to do is see the good in them, *for them*, and you will stoke their fire.

Fires can hardly pass a mirror and not look at themselves in it. This includes all reflective surfaces, like streams, metallic refrigerators, the shiny surface of a phone—who do you think invented pocket vanity mirrors? A Fire person, no doubt. This isn't really narcissism but more like the need to fit in. They need to feel lovable and have the unfortunate belief that ugly equates to unlovable or rejection.

If Fire feels unattractive, they believe you won't receive the love they have to offer. If you're really not attracted to your Fire lover, this is a major problem in the relationship for both of you. Let's admit it: their appearance is probably what made you attracted to them in the first place. If that attraction disappears, they feel they've failed in their mission to share their love with you. If you're no longer attracted to your Fire lover, it's time to let them go because they can't be themselves unless they feel beautiful to you. That lack of interest is like throwing the wet blanket on a roaring blaze. Can you hear that noise of the squelched Fire? Tsssssssssssssst . . .

A Fire in this situation may even begin to live the part of being rejected and feeling ugly. If they feel their partner thinks they're not the right shape, they let themselves go. They may gain more weight and stop caring about their clothes. They lose touch with their inner beauty and their outer beauty reflects that as well.

Fires are vulnerable, but don't mistake this for weakness; they're one of the strongest Elements. When Fire is doing well, expect them to have a lot of strong opinions about all aspects of life. The heart in Chinese Medicine is called the "Supreme Controller." There are different kinds of Fires: some are very controlling, others are a bit less so, but all Fires like to feel in control of their loved ones. This is different than Wood's delegation behavior; it's more like needing to make plans and pack the day with as many things to do as possible whether it's realistic or not. They see all the amazing things that could be done in a day, and they want to do it all. So they're constantly asking everyone around them to go somewhere or do something with them. They don't give orders, but they smile sweetly and coerce, and then get their way. Often it's hard to resist a Fire's magnetism and warmth. That's the way of the Fire.

You can fight the Supreme Controller if you want, but they will learn your weaknesses in the end. You could call it manipulative, which is partially true. But really they want you to be happy, and they're constantly compromising to find a way for *everyone* to be happy, including themselves and the person they just met five minutes ago—their new BFF! It's good to remember that your happiness in the relationship is paramount to Fires. And they would never sacrifice that for any of their schemes. You can easily explain why some scenario would make you very unhappy and watch Fire do tap dances to find a compromise that makes you happy. They want everyone to be happy all the time, 24-7.

Remember too that Fires love knowledge. So they can be the know-it-alls, along with their Wood and Earth counterparts. It can be a bit pedantic at times. As a partner of a Fire, a sense of humor about their knowledge is helpful. They love it when you love their foibles as well as their strengths. (Actually, they're ecstatic when you love them for anything at all!) So instead of feeling resentment about the constant stream of know-it-all comments, you can play with them, tease them gently, and at the same time, take them seriously when clearly their knowledge is helpful in a given moment. Fires love to work on their weaknesses, so there's a lot of ability to change and learn.

They Don't Know How to Say No

Other Elements might say to them: "Why do you care so much? Why do you have to go to every party you're invited to?" And they may not have an answer, but the underlying truth is, whether they know it or not, they want to share the joy and light inside them with the world. Oh, and they love parties too.

They love fiercely. They've put their trust in you as their partner. This means they wear their hearts on their sleeves around you and are more vulnerable to your meanness than when they're out in the world with other people. When you hurt their feelings (and often this happens by mistake on your part), their beautiful open hearts suddenly slam shut—not a good thing for you. A Fire who has a closed heart can be pouty, cranky, irritable, or cry incessantly…and they may not tell you why or what you did wrong. It takes a lot for a Fire who really loves you to say something hurtful. What they tend to do is be mean with a smile on their face. This can be interpreted as passive-aggressive. It really is, but we're trying to be nice here. They may not even know their hearts are closed and they're upset. They're trying to be happy and nice, but the anger and pain they feel inside seeps out in their words.

When your Fire partner is behaving oddly in any of these ways, it's time to stop everything and give them some loving. Don't be surprised if they burst into tears when you do this. Really, it's a good thing! Whenever their hearts begin to open back up, it often comes with tears. When the tears have stopped and that genuine smile returns to their face, you've succeeded. Their hearts are open again, you can connect, and you can return to life lived happily ever after until the next time you mistakenly hurt them. When, not if, that happens, repeat the above remedy and dish out the love again. The benefit of this kind of relationship is you will experience a beautiful heart connection that you will get with no other Element. Remember, Fire is all about love in all its wonderful forms.

Accepting Earth:
A Force to Be Reckoned With

If your partner is Earth, you need to be connected and present. You have to be willing to talk about your emotions and listen to your Earth partner talk about theirs. You also have to come to terms with the fact that you can't hide anything from them. They will sniff out the truth like a bloodhound. Earth is the Sherlock Holmes of the Elements. They will find out how, why, and when every time. No chance you can pull the wool over these Earthly eyes. It's just not going to happen.

Family is very important to Earth. To keep Earth happy, you need to take on and connect with their families like they're your own. You have to be invested in their family and all its idiosyncrasies. Even if they claim that they're not into their families, they are; it just means they're entwined with their family's dramas to a greater degree. In that situation, nothing makes an Earth happier than when their partner goes willingly to family events with them.

If you're partnered with Earth, count yourself lucky to receive all the gifts your partner offers. But be wary and careful. If they are angry, they can easily become full of resentment. It could rear its ugly head from time to time in a moment's notice. That's when they hold back their gifts purposely, and it's not pretty. (Not to mention that sex is usually at the top of the withheld gift list!) If your partner is Earth, you need to pull enough of your own weight (a fraction of the truckload of weight your Earth partner is probably pulling) so that Earth thinks you actually care about the partnership and all they do.

When Earth gets disappointed, they are quick to point out deficiencies—theirs and yours. It's easy to feel bruised and battered by a disappointed Earth. They could be the emotional steamrollers in the Elemental world. They are the problem solvers, which means, they see problems. They want to help fix them. Maybe they need to go to a workshop to learn how to fix it, or they'll buy a book like—hmm, maybe a book like *this* one. They don't give up. They'll keep working on solving the problem as long as it takes.

Try not to think of them as mean or cranky. They just want to solve the problems and create positive change, no matter what. If you feel defensive about how they point out what they see as wrong, try not to take it personally. They just want you to work with them. First, they will want you to admit that there are problems. Don't even try to deny them (remember they are the bloodhounds on the scent of truth). If life happens, then problems happen; they are natural.

Solutions are, too. When you work together to solve problems, you are a team, a unit, working out issues together. That is when Earth is smiling, happy, and caring.

They're always improving something. This means you have to care that they care about problems, even if you don't care. You might think something they're working on is a waste of time. But take the time anyway to ask them questions ... be involved, join them. They feel deeply connected to you when you're both working together to make your relationship that much better.

If you've made a mistake that has made them feel very unsafe or uncared-for, you're going to have to understand that they can forgive but they'll never forget. This lack of forgetting means twenty-five years from now, they might bring up that time when you [insert your worst transgression here]. It may feel harsh, and it can be. How can you move on from something you might be embarrassed about if they rehash it over and over?

The airing of grievances can be a deal-breaker for some couples, but it helps to understand why Earths do this. Earth wants to understand *everything*. They are trying to understand you constantly. The only reason they bring it up again is that they still don't understand your motivation. If you can really help them understand, then true forgiveness can come. This means that they formed an opinion of you based on their observations—an opinion that may have lasted more than twenty-five years! It's up to you to help them change a bad idea; otherwise you'll live that bad rap for the rest of your relationship. Maybe this was a wrong assumption in the first place, maybe a simple miscommunication, or maybe you have actually *changed* after all these years! It's up to you to help them alter their opinion of you. You have some explaining to do, even if it seems so old and not important to you. It's huge for them.

The other thing you need to realize about your Earth partner is that life is pretty slow-paced. It takes them a long time to do certain tasks. Normally they compensate for this by doing a lot of preparation before an event so that on the day of the event, things go quickly and smoothly. They like to make it look easy. But with raising the children or the stresses of a job, they might feel overwhelmed and unable to properly prepare in advance. It might be getting out of the house for a picnic (all the food that needs to be packed takes time). Or it might be putting something together at home like a new screen house (yes, Earth has to read every line of the instruction manual). Other times they do things rather fast, but those are the routine things (cleaning the house, school lunches, weeding the garden). They love their routines. But if they are doing something new, there's a lot of analysis that has to happen for them to assimilate it into one of their tasks or chores.

Patience is the best virtue to have if you want to live and love Earth. You have to develop patience to be with Earth because you're going to be waiting... *a lot.* Just try shopping together. If you're a fast shopper and your partner is Earth, you're probably used to waiting around. They read the labels, look at every item on the shelf methodically to pick the one that is perfect. All this careful attention takes time, and why rush? If that's okay with you, then there's no problem. But if you resent it constantly, then you'll be forever trying to move Earth along, and a lot of bickering will ensue. You can develop coping strategies... have a book to read, play a game on your phone, wait in the car patiently and respectfully, or whatever you need to do to allow Earth to be slow and let them enjoy what they are doing for the good of the family.

You can also work with Earth on the things that matter to you. For example, you can ask them to be speedier when you really need them to move. They love to solve problems that you identify without blame or shame. They're constantly asking everyone else to make changes to improve relationships. If you actually initiate problem-solving, that can make them very happy. It means you're invested and want to really try to improve together. Nothing could be better than that. Your desire to *try* is almost better than the solution itself.

Accepting Metal: The Cutting Edge

If you're partnered with Metal, you need to want to dive deep into abstract thoughts and ideas at times. When you listen to these philosophical discussions, you let the thoughts breathe, give them space, ponder, and marinate. Metals really like to talk a lot with the right people. If you're willing to move beyond small talk, you'll be blessed with very stimulating conversation with your Metal partner. Oddly, some couples have a communication breakdown, and the non-Metal partner may complain that their partner never talks and keeps everything to themselves. The Metal partner doesn't have trouble talking about interesting topics, but they'll wait to see if you truly want to listen before they open up on more important or deeper issues. This means you have to be willing to connect with them before the conversation can really begin to forge ahead.

Metals can be quick to judge a situation and decide that there's only one way to do a project. They are the not out-of-the-box thinkers like Wood when it comes to rules and regulations; however, they are very out-of-the-box visionaries when it comes to things like art, music, and abstract ideas. Often they see limitations everywhere. They are the "I can't do that" people. Or they are the ones who might say, "you can't do that." They may point out often that you're about to or have crossed the line—that something you're doing isn't acceptable for some reason (socially, legally, or ethically). And there's really no arguing that point with Metal. Rules are rules. There are no gray areas. Like the scales of justice, it's right or it's wrong.

When your Metal partner thinks something you want to do is wrong and you shouldn't do it, it's important to understand that they aren't judging you, they're judging your *actions.* They really mostly see things in black and white. They don't think you can fudge anything. Through the Five Elements, you can learn to lighten the severity of Metal by being playful with them. Metals have a wonderful sense of humor. If you as a couple understand that the judge is a very useful role in life, you can accept this aspect in your partner and respect and honor it. In fact, they often avert major disasters by pointing out the significant risks in whatever you're about to do. Even if you decide to go ahead, you may adjust your course accordingly to avert that potential disaster, thankful for the Metal-ing of your Metal.

You can also help your Metal partner accept that there are actually other ways of doing things in life, including bending the rules once in awhile. You may see something they could do differently, maybe a creative solution to a problem, for example. They'll shoot it down at first. But after some discussion, they can sometimes see the wisdom in changing the rules slightly and may come around to your way of thinking. It can happen, honest!

Metals generally appear as though they're sitting back and watching the world peacefully, but often when they are frustrated, they can build up negative feelings about what's going on in the world. They might be annoyed by any one of the hundreds of things they see. And let's face it, there are a lot of injustices in the world, and Metal sees them all. But instead of commenting on it or telling someone, they hold that annoyance and frustration inside. As life continues on around them, they have more and more grievances they're quietly holding on to. They especially struggle with issues of authority or respect. When they are supposed to be deferential to someone (a parent or teacher) who is clearly out of line, they really struggle. And instead of saying anything, they hold that emotion, feeling like a champagne bottle ready to pop. What puts them over the edge depends on how big the frustrations or the length of time without popping their cork, so to speak.

You can imagine that holding in all these feelings creates an overall problem. Eventually this builds up until they become angry (it actually takes a lot to get them to this point, though). These same peaceful, mellow Metals change into short-tempered people. Or they end up blowing up at the person they are upset with in a not-so-nice way, even destroying relationships in the process.

Over time, Metal can become extremely pessimistic about everything and may feel safe enough to share that information with their partner. If it's about a boss or someone who doesn't affect you directly, you may hear the stories over and over. But if Metal is upset with you even briefly, Metal can swiftly chop you down (especially if you're a Wood tree—which is often a target for Metal).

If your Metal partner's difficulties are making life at home unbearable, it's time to discuss what's really going on with them. In some cases, Metals are quite relieved when they hear that it's normal for Metal to avoid confronting people for a long time. They were afraid to speak in the first place in case the vehemence they are holding inside comes out. They really are nice people and don't want to cause trouble.

In order to have a happy peaceful Metal partner, you can help your lover communicate with the people they are truly angry at without blowing up at them. Walk through scenarios of dialog with them, for example, ways to talk to their boss that won't result in getting fired. Think of it as relieving some of the pressure in the champagne bottle. Perhaps, you can help them develop strategies of what to dialog. And if Metal is still angry with you, discuss that it's important to talk about that right away and not let things fester or build up inside. Develop strategies for the two of you to have very open, unafraid conversations without guilt or blame. Whatever your feelings are, negative or positive, learn to talk about them before they become explosive

Accepting Water: Keeping Your Head Above Water

If you're partnered with Water, you need to identify some key factors to keep things moving in the right direction. Is your Water partner mostly like a tide pool or more like a waterfall or perhaps somewhere in between? Pooling Waters, as we like to call them, tend to be a bit more messy and mostly content with their messiness. Gushing Waters tend to be the opposite (neater, sometimes obsessively) and overly ambitious, which might mean focusing on a particular task with high, focused energy.

For most Water types, at the beginning of a really good relationship they are totally excited about you and very hyper-focused on your life. Remember they are intense about everything, including a new lover. This feels really great and fulfilling to both of you. But eventually, as time passes, something else may pique their interest. Uh-oh! Why did your Water lover just disappear? Where did they go? If you suddenly feel a bit abandoned or lonely, this is normal. It's just that your Water is suddenly focused intensely on something else and not really forgetting about you. This loneliness might cause trouble in some relationships. Some people really desire a partner who is totally present with them and involved in their life pretty much all the time. Waters tend to disappear into other interests and projects only to resurface again later.

Both partners can learn to understand and accept this fact and work with it. You need to know that your Water partner will be focused on you again soon. One woman said her husband buries himself in his work for weeks at a time, then one day will come home and she knows they're going to make love for the next five days. Once she discovered this cycle and accepted it, she was fine with it. Others aren't so fine with it. They need someone there all the time. The Water partner may have to learn to put down their new excitement and be present with their partner at the end of each day, to touch base, connect and show some interest in them. With some adjustments and self-awareness, they can perhaps learn to do that on a fairly regular basis.

Living with Water can be a lot of fun, but living with the messier types of Water, you may need to adjust if you want to share a household together. It's as if they spill out all over the place, endlessly. Many times this is a deal-breaker for couples. The non-Water person just feels buried by the constant clutter and cannot adjust to this near constant state of messiness and organizational chaos. Some couples have developed wonderful strategies for dealing with this aspect of Water, such as having areas of the house where Water is allowed to spill out and can be messy. Many a garage, shed, back room, or closet has been designated for the collection of stuff a Water person can accumulate over time. With a non-judgmental approach, Water can feel normal and not guilty or blamed for their natural tendencies to just spread out. From that no-blaming place, you can find ways to contain Water, like giving them organizing spaces to put stuff into. It's about containment and not overpowering them, breaking their will, or even threatening them. When they come home, they need a place to put everything near the door—to drop their day's loot of stuff. Keys, glasses, change, mail, bags, packages ... the list can get quite long.

They also love to collect things, many things—different sets of things and interests. Over time this can be a burden to many. A garage or shed may need to be dedicated to your Water partner as their acquisitions grow. Sheds were surely invented for Waters! Ever expanding, Water will continue to spread and spread.

For the rushing river types of Water, you may find your partner is quite neat. But they never slow down! The have the energy of a never ending river that just goes and goes, the energizer bunny of the Elemental world. They just keep going and going and going. They're constantly anticipating what needs to be done. But even the neat Waters may also collect things that need a lot of space to hold their acquisitions.

Are you the talkative type? Love to talk about all your emotions and emotional needs on a fairly regular basis? Well, this could be an issue because you might *not* be able to talk about these kinds of things with your Water partner. Both of you have to accept that there is a time and place to discuss these things. Water wants to be happy in the present moment. They don't like when you dredge up negative issues from the past. Maybe they were upset about something a little while ago (it's fine to talk about it then), and now they've put it out of their minds and are enjoying a nice meal with you. But then you're bringing up something that made them sad and want to cry. In their minds, they might be wondering why you would ruin dinner by talking about the past and making them upset now; it just doesn't make sense to them. And you certainly don't need to talk before being intimate, oh no. First be in the moment physically, and then later at an appropriate time, discuss what you need to. This can be a big hurdle for many people to understand and accept.

Waters often have to learn and appreciate that some partners need to actually talk about emotions and feelings. You can make small agreements to talk at specific times of the day or go to a specific place together with the purpose of talking and exploring thoughts about what is bothering you. Perhaps, you can develop a better habit of talking together through the acceptance of loving the now moment and be able to be joyfully swept away in the wonderful immediateness of Water.

Two Sides to Every Coin

What's the point of all this? Why go over all the not-so-pretty challenges of being with each Element? Well, we feel the main goal of this book is to learn as much as you can about yourself, so you can start to love yourself even more. Learning about what you really want directly relates to finding the person you want to spend your life with. Once you understand yourself and find the love of your life, then how do you keep it? You really have to learn to accept your partner for who they truly are. As well, they must do the same with you. You both may learn things and become aware of things you never even saw in each other before. Your partner doesn't have to do things exactly like you would or be exactly like you. You can be very different and still be very much in love.

Understanding and loving the differences in each other is a beautiful thing. You may have been trying to convince your partner to do things your way for years, and it just isn't working anymore and now you know why! Perhaps it's time to accept that you have two different ways of doing things and you have two choices. Work on it with them or not. It is that simple. And once you can accept the way your partner is, you can move into having a more fulfilling relationship for both of you.

The majority of relationship difficulties come from Control Cycle issues. One Element emotionally shuts down the other element, all the time. Over time, this can be defeating, and these patterns are hard to break. Seeing and understanding this can be the information you need to start new thought patterns, new ways of communicating and loving each other.

If you find yourself in a Control Cycle relationship (Metal/Wood, Wood/Earth, Earth/Water, Water/Fire, Fire/Metal), then it's time to evaluate how you can heal those negative dynamics and move into a more positive space. The "Control" of the cycle refers to the one Element unconsciously controlling the other so they don't get out of hand. In the grand scheme of things, this is a very positive force. For example, Water needs containment from Earth or it will flood everything. Overgrown Wood needs pruning by Metal or it will become wild and untamed. Out of control Fire needs to be doused by Water or it will consume everything in sight. Metal needs melting and tempering with Fire to transform its states. Wood nourishes and secures the Earth, preventing natural disasters like mud slides and dry dust storms.

The challenges arise when the person being controlled feels like their destiny is being thwarted by an overly controlling partner. They literally can't fulfill their mission because the one they love is constantly shutting them down. They may even begin to verbally attack their partner out of frustration. In Chinese Medicine, the reverse of the Control Cycle is called the Insulting Cycle. Your partner may find the only way they can assert their will in the relationship is by being literally insulting to you.

For example, take Fire and Metal. The exuberance of Fire shuts down Metal. Fire cuts Metal off when they're speaking and can constantly talk over them. Metal ends up feeling angry and shut off. Fire often has great ideas, but Metal might end up resisting them as a result of not having a fair say in the matter. In contrast, Metals can be quite talkative with other Metals and be extremely optimistic about life. Finding the balance and equality with each partner having a voice would help this combination.

In any Control Cycle relationship that is struggling, the Controller has to learn to ease off and let the other person be themselves. The Controlled person needs to learn to assert themselves lovingly in the relationship and not let their partner do everything.

Stealing Their Thunder

Every relationship takes work. Nourishing Cycle relationships (Wood/Fire, Fire/Earth, Earth/Metal, Metal/Water, and Water/Wood) are often very compatible. When couples struggle in a Nourishing Cycle Relationship, it's usually because they don't really understand the gifts and weakness of each other's Element, and they try to change them or control them.

Nourishing relationships have a "parent" energy and a "child" energy. The parent might tell the child what to do, but it's done in a way that's much more harmonious than in a Control Cycle relationship. The "child" energy receives the "parenting" energy very well. This can be easier for some couples, but others can struggle with this energy dynamic due to misunderstandings or miscommunications that can occur.

The difficulties often happen when the "Parent" energy person is struggling. The "Parent" Element may not want to show weakness because parents feel like they should be strong for their loved ones. And the "Child" can struggle in feeling like they have to fix it quickly because the parent is supposed to be well and happy. Instead of helping the sick "Parent" when they're down, the "Child" can end up demanding all the attention. This obviously feels terrible for the "Parent." And sometimes when great difficulties arise, it can cause a break up. Accepting this dynamic and laughing about it in the moment can really shift things and promote healing.

Sometimes Nourishing Cycle relationships struggle because they simply don't understand their differences. For example, in a Fire/Earth relationship, Earth needs to understand that Fire is vulnerable. Earth likes to get to the truth and fix problems. And they aren't always nice about it. The result is Fire can take it very badly and begin to feel shut down, bad about themselves, and not even tell the Earth partner what's going on. Thus a pattern can begin to develop. Fire behaves less and less competently, and Earth gets more and more upset (because the "Parent" energy is supposed to be more competent and involved). The whole reason Earth wanted to be with Fire was because they were attracted to their competence and warmth. As this worsens, Earth may begin to resent when Fire shuts down and is no longer partnering.

To heal this dynamic, the couple needs better communication about past events. Earth needs to understand why Fire did the things they did so forgiveness can come.

Broken but Very Repairable

Becoming aware of these patterns is the first step on the road to romantic recovery. The Five Elements helps you both accept your unconscious dynamics and learn how to change them to more positive interactions. You both have to learn to overcome your default patterns in life.

Each of you lives according to your Elemental Energy type, but you don't have to do it that way all the time. Remember, you are all Five Elements. You can learn new techniques that encourage your partner to be more authentic.

Conclusion:
Freedom to Fly

....

"Do or do not. There is no try."
Yoda, Star Wars

....

Learning and living the Five Elements opens your eyes to new ways of seeing things and experiencing life—your life and everything around you. It is exciting to see the world with new eyes, even if this is ancient knowledge. This new way of seeing the world can create freedom in your life...you now have a choice of how to view your life on an energetic level.

Think about it. All your life, every time a particular event occurs, you behaved a certain way. Not only that, you believed this is the best way or the only way to behave. Perhaps you wanted to act or react differently but didn't know how. Then you beat yourself up over your choices. You may feel like you can't change this behavior even if you want to.

The Chinese philosophy behind the Five Elements is that first you accept who you are so you can understand your gifts to the world. Knowing your Element helps you celebrate and forgive yourself simultaneously. You do the things you do for a reason. Your Elemental Energy type dictates what you do naturally. The combination of your Elemental Energies makes you unique in who you are! You can develop the freedom to act or react the way you want to. You can even love the way you want. You are the one true thing that you can change and love. Love yourself and the world will also love you.

The Fab Five

So, what is your gift?

If you are Wood, you have the emotion of *anger*, which really translates better as *assertiveness*. You have the ability to make change happen in the world. Acting assertively on your frustrations in healthy and positive ways causes you to make changes. And that's the gift of Wood to the world.

If you are Fire, you are about *joy* and *contentment*. You can turn anything bad into something wonderfully good. You give the world laughter and fun, and not taking things so seriously. Your bright shining light that comes from within highlights this joy and contentment in the world.

If you are Earth, you give the world *sympathy*, which is better translated as *thought* and *understanding*. This is nothing like pity or sappy sympathy. It's the desire to deeply know another person, to truly get them. The lessons you teach and share are valuable and meaningful to the world.

If you are Metal, you give the world *appreciation and connection.* You have the emotion of *grief,* which can sometimes be better translated as *nostalgia.* It's the sense of connection with things that ephemeral and fleeting in life and appreciating them even more so because they are brief. Your lifetime is essentially a brief blip of time in eternity. Every being is precious. The cosmic connections you show the rest of us is inspiring and calming.

If you are Water, you give the world *intensity.* You have the emotion of *fear,* which may be better translated as a state of *anticipation.* You live completely in the now moment, ready to be fully involved with a surging power. And to be that intense, you have to live in quiet and peacefulness, prepared for anything. That unpredictability and love of adventure, which can take many forms, leaves us all wanting more excitement in our lives.

DaZed and ConfuZed?

This book can seemingly have the effect of making you feel dazed and confused after reading it for the first time. We hope everyone will read it many times (except Wood, whom we know will value the information but probably will only read it once) and use this information as a guide. It's a book that really offers you solutions and reference tools to many relationship issues in life. However, it takes some time to digest it and apply it to your life. So go easy on yourself: take baby steps, then leaps and bounds, and then have the courage to learn to fly. This is your life, and you really can do what you want with it!

Change Comes from Within

Look at the positive and negative aspects of your Elements. Once you realize that others have the same gifts and drawbacks, can you accept yourself and even your faults? If so, then what do you want to change? From a place of acceptance, the Chinese believe you can actually change—not because you hate yourself, but because you love yourself and have the power to grow and be more evolved. To change, you have to watch your habits and behaviors over periods of time—understanding what (or who) triggers your reactions. Once you see how it all works with yourself, you can begin to make changes in the patterns you've developed. Every time a trigger occurs, your awareness of it allows you to make a choice. These kinds of changes take time.

When you look at your relationship with a partner, seeing these changes is very rewarding (and illuminating). If a behavior of yours causes strain in your relationship, then through your acceptance and willingness to change, you can do it differently. You can try to move gently in a new direction. Slow change is, for many, the best way to grow.

Changing yourself may help heal very old patterns between you and your partner. Chapter eleven described this process in detail, so we suggest you and your partner read it together and talk about it. Doing so without blame or shame can be a first step to rediscovering the love you once had.

Talking the Talk, Walking the Walk

Life is a path of self-discovery, and it's time you started. Heck, you're probably way overdue! It's sometimes fun, sometimes not so fun when we do the whole self-examination thing. The Five Elements offers an amazing way to find out about yourself and your life on so many levels. It is worth the effort. How many books, videos, and gurus have told us over and over all the things that are wrong with us? How many articles have been written on fixing what is broken or wrong in relationships? Who's telling us what's right with us? The Five Elements is one of the most positive and effective ways to study human behavior. We've written this book to create acceptance and forgiveness rather than identifying problems and blaming personality traits. We want to end the blame game so many couples struggle with.

Beyond the Basics

If you're still craving more, you're in luck! This book only scratches the surface. Many Daoists believe we are eternal beings, meaning that our spirit has many lifetimes to live and that we are on a journey of learning from lifetime to lifetime. Daoists believe we choose our parents and the events of our life prior to being born so that we can have a particular learning experience. Ultimately the goal of this learning is to transcend this reality. But what does that mean?

All right, how about this? We love to tell this tale when explaining transcending reality. It's simple but has blown people's minds for centuries: an old Daoist sage wrote about a butterfly who was dreaming it was a man, but then woke up and was the man, who thought he was dreaming of being a butterfly. Which was it?

Here, reality is an illusion, a dream. That means we are incarnated to live experiences that aren't really real at all. Daoists believe that despite this all being an illusion, we must still experience life fully. They don't believe the answer is to spend your life detached and alone in a cave, closed off from emotions. They think it's through our emotions that we discover ourselves. This is the path of becoming a sage, which starts with knowing yourself and your Element. Then you need to learn all the nuances of each Element within yourself. When you learn to shift your Elemental Energy at any moment, you can experience life as if you are another Elemental type. Once you can be all Five Elements in yourself, you can transcend the illusion and step into the source of all, the Dao.

Life is about experiences, including sharing them with your loved ones. Relationship is one of life's fundamental components. You can try to avoid it, but it will come knocking at your door when you least expect it. So go ahead, open the door—kick it down if you want! Ahead of you is an entryway to your own heart through relationships.